So, You Want To Be A Full-Time RVer?

Published By

John and Kathy Huggins

Forward

This book is and will be a work in progress. We have put down as much of our experience and knowledge as we can remember and research, but there is so much about the RV lifestyle to tell. We wrote the most about the things we know and have experienced. We have said many times, "We are experienced, but not experts". Although we are full-timers, the information applies to part time RVers as well

We want to especially thank the loyal listeners of our podcast, "Living the RV Dream". The "you should write a book" talk started several years ago. At that time, writing a book was the farthest thing from our minds. We were working and travelling as well as keeping up a weekly one hour radio show. Recently, we received a flurry of e-mails asking us again to publish the stuff we talk about on the show. So here you are folks. We give you our labor of love for the last eight months. We believe you will think it was worth the wait.

We want to thank our son Steve who first asked us to do an RV radio show. To Jim Bathurst, author of "Cat on a Leash" and very thorough editor and proofreader, go our sincere thanks. To our daughter in law Dr. Shelley Huggins who helped with proofreading, thank you for taking time away from our grandchildren to do this for us. We give a special thank you to Nick and Terry Russell. Nick is the author and editor of "The Gypsy Journal" and bestselling author of the "Big Lake" series of books. Nick, you gave us the encouragement to do this project and shared your knowledge of e-publishing. You also took time out of your busy schedule to be one of our proofreaders.

To our Lord and Savior Jesus Christ go all the glory.

Table of Contents

Chapter 1 Are You Out of Your Mind?

Kathy and I dreamed about full-timing for years before we even knew it or did anything about it. We would be driving on the interstate and see a big coach or fifth-wheel trailer and we would think and say together, "That will be us some day". We were convinced even then that touring the country in a big rig was the best way to travel. We didn't even imagine we could do it as a full-time lifestyle.

Can you imagine how we felt after we joyously sold our house and most of the stuff in it and moved into our new-to-us RV for a great adventure and lifestyle change and heard "Are you out of your mind?" Unfortunately, this seemed to be the attitude of a lot of the people we know and love when we made the announcement. Those folks have a really high resistance to change. So many people are quite content and happy to live in the same house in the same town with the same people around them for their entire lives. That is perfectly fine for them and we don't want to change them. When someone in their circle decides to break away from that comfort zone, however, they find it hard to understand. You will be asked, "How in the world can you live 24/7 in that tin can?" "You'll go stir crazy and kill each other!" "How will you pay your bills?" and "How will you get your mail?" I can think of many other similar comments, but you get the point. Take heart my friend, because they will never feel the freedom of the open road. They won't see this country like you will. They won't do new things and meet new friends like you will every time you fire up your rig and hit the road for someplace new.

One common issue is that one spouse or partner is ready to jump into this lifestyle, sell everything, buy a rig and hit the open road, while the other has serious doubts. Often one or the other has serious issues with leaving their home and most of their belongings behind. If you live close to family, children and grandchildren, it can be hard to cut those ties. In some severe cases, the conflicts of a full-time lifestyle will not work for those folks. We aren't qualified to give advice to help solve these conflicts. It's unfortunate, but this lifestyle isn't for everyone. Possibly you might want to try "Long Timing" or extended trips away from your sticks and bricks house before you jump off the ledge into full-timing.

One of the questions that was asked was "Won't you get on each other's nerves and argue and fight?" The answer is a qualified "sometimes". Hopefully, you and your partner have given a lot of thought to living 24/7 in a hallway. No matter the type of RV, from small travel trailer to a 45 foot luxury motor home, all of them are narrow hallways. The best you can expect is about four hundred and fifty square feet, and that is exceptional. It won't take long and that space will shrink in on you unless you get your head(s) around it. We all need personal space and RVing is no exception. You can go outside, or to one end of your unit, but make sure you both realize the need for some "alone" time.

I don't want to start off with doom and gloom, but this is a reality. Since this lifestyle is not for everyone, realizing and planning for any the possible downsides can help this experience to be the most rewarding thing you have ever done. Kathy and I were married for thirty-eight years before we set out full-timing. We knew which buttons not to push so as to avoid conflict. We now live closely together in less than 400 square feet and there are certainly situations where we don't agree with one another. We have found the best cure is some alone time to do our own thing without one another. Kathy needs a certain amount of "Kathy" time to herself to read, or shop, or even think without me and I realize that. Consequently, we avoid most serious fights and arguments.

The closest experience most folks have probably had to this type of close living is when they go on a vacation. They'll get on a plane or in the car and travel somewhere and check into a motel. Who knows who slept in that bed last and what did they leave behind? On the other hand, we can go far beyond airports and motels and restaurants. We sleep in our own bed and cook our food if we want to. We can even stay off the grid if we desire.

It took us almost a year to realize that we were embarking on a new and exciting **Lifestyle**, not an extended vacation. Initially, we fell into the unending vacation trap when we started out full- time. We felt we had to go, go, go, and see everything and do everything all in the first several months. In our case, this "Express Touring" lasted for the first year. We also spent as much money in that year as in the next three! We were moving so fast, we only cherry picked the highlights of the part of our beautiful country we happened to be in. We finally realized we had plenty of time to see

13

things and we could return to see and do things we missed the first time. A good case in point is our love of the Black Hills of South Dakota. We have spent four summers there and I don't believe we've seen it all yet. It's that way all over the country. As stated above, we cherry picked the high points in our travels, but there would have been so much more to see had we stayed longer.

We started the Living the RV Dream radio show four years into full-timing, and it was then that we realized we were truly living a very wonderful and special lifestyle. But, that is the beauty of it. You have the freedom to do what you want to do and when you want to do it. It's your choice. You can plan a trip down to the hour with all stops booked and attractions planned in advance; or you can have your plans set in Jell-O like we do. We'll discuss plans and goals in detail later on.

Something that came as a surprise were the many new friends we have made while traveling and during our volunteering and workamping assignments. We meet people with similar experience and lifetime friendships result. This probably would never happen in our former insulated life in a sticks and brick house where we moved in a small circle of family and friends. Because we share this unique lifestyle, we bond much more quickly than before. Thanks to e-mail and social media, we continue to keep in touch. We may not see someone for a year or more, but when we meet again in some other place on the map, that friendship is still strong and it becomes a joyous homecoming.

Of course the naysayers had many other questions like "How will you ever learn to drive that great big thing?" and a host of other questions. We couldn't answer some of these at first. Well, most will be revealed and much, much more as you read this book. I want to emphasize that Kathy and I are NOT experts in this RV lifestyle, but after more than 7 years on the road, we are experienced and we have had much trial and error to get to good answers. Those are the Lessons Learned at the end of the book. We are so glad you are joining us in this book endeavor and we invite you to join us on our weekly RV radio show on the internet called "Living the RV Dream". Check out our website at http://www.livingthervdream.com .

Chapter 2 Do Your Homework

The very first thing to do when contemplating either the full-time or part-time RV lifestyle is a fair amount of what we call "homework" to arrive at good decisions. Homework starts with deciding what kind of lifestyle you will live. Do you love NASCAR, rodeos, visiting family, being a snowbird, seeing the country and its natural beauty? Perhaps you enjoy traveling around and doing volunteer work at churches or maybe Habitat for Humanity. That might determine what type of rig will be best for your lifestyle. You will have to figure out how you will handle your mail and bills. Do you know how you will finance this dream? You must do at least a preliminary budget to decide what you can afford. Will you have adequate healthcare insurance? How will you communicate with people? Have you thought about what you will do with your "stuff"? All this and more goes into the "Homework" part of getting ready to be RVers.

We started our homework at the local library. We read every book on RVing. Some were good and informative and some were not. Some talked about current RVing information and some were old and outdated. Various internet sites led us to more information and helped us to ask better questions. We looked at the manufacturer's web sites and we went to the Florida RV Super show and met up with two couples who were members of the Escapees RV Club. They talked to us for more than an hour and a half about full-time RVing. We didn't even know what that was but it sounded exciting. Of course, we asked what the down side was; they paused and pondered the question and then like a choir they said "we should have done it ten years sooner".

OK, we were hooked, but there was still a lot more to investigate. We also looked around at all the different RVs and got their brochures to take home and study, and we took lots of pictures. John checked the underneath space and I pretended that I was living in the RV and made dinner and tried to make the bed. We must have walked twenty miles and looked into a hundred RVs. We then went to the local RV dealers within a hundred miles of our home. Many salesmen were informative and some were not. It helped us to decide on a motor home for the lifestyle we were planning on living, instead of a 5th wheel or a travel trailer. John talked to service managers to find out which brands needed more service than others. We visited local campgrounds and talked with campers about their RVs and about their lifestyle. Some were full-timers and were really enjoying it, some were long timers who were gone from their homes for four to ten months at a time, and some were camping almost every weekend. They all enjoyed the camping lifestyle they had chosen. We learned what they liked about campgrounds and what they looked for when choosing the campground. They told us some horror stories about camping but they still loved it and were very informative.

We started to subscribe to Motorhome magazine and the Escapees magazine and read them from cover to cover. Gleaning all the information we could, we knew we needed to make the best decision possible. Buying a motor home is expensive and we wanted to make the best decision for us. We finally decided on a motor home and we picked out three different models that we liked when we were ready to buy. This process took almost two years but that time was well spent. We have had our motor home for seven years and we still like it a lot.

Chapter 3 Should I Change My State of Residence?

When Kathy and I started on the full-time adventure, we were unaware of the advantage of selecting a state for domicile purposes. We were in Florida and paid no state taxes and we thought that was enough. Not so! We paid seven percent sales tax on the motor home purchase. That was a sizeable chunk of money we could have used for better purpose. We realized there were other possibilities when we were researching mail forwarding services. We went to the website of Alternative Resources http://www.alternativeresources.net/ and all the advantages of South Dakota residence were listed. At that point we purchased "Choosing Your RV Home Base" from Roundabout Publications at Camping World. Now it is available at Amazon.com and at www.rvbookstore.com . This book is a must have if you are just starting out full-timing.

In it we found state by state listings of: financial liability by state; federal taxes for full-timers; state retirement exemptions; tax advantages of each state; vehicle licensing registration specifics; and voting rules and requirements. We were able to compare states and wrote down the things that were important to us. At the end of this process, we chose South Dakota for no state income taxes, low vehicle insurance and registration, and very friendly probate laws.

The RV lifestyle gives us the unique opportunity to choose any state to call "home". For anyone considering the full-time RV lifestyle, a state to establish a home base can be quite important and there are several factors that must be considered. Among the most important issues for full-timers are taxes, insurance, and RV fees. Which states have the best income tax advantages? Which states offer the best rates on RV registration, including annual vehicle taxes? If you pick the wrong state to establish an official residence, it could result in your spending thousands of dollars a year that could be saved by establishing a home base elsewhere. And just how does a full-timer establish an official residency? Is it enough to simply rent a post office box? I don't think so.

As soon as we arrived in South Dakota, we established a mailing address using a mail forwarding service. Then we surrendered our Florida driver's licenses and got South Dakota ones. Next, we went to an insurance office and got the lower priced South Dakota insurance for our car and motor home. The car insurance was half of the Florida rate. Our last stop was at the courthouse for vehicle registration for new license plates for both vehicles. That was much less expensive also. We also registered to vote in South Dakota. Because we travel so much, we do not vote in local elections and use absentee ballots for federal elections. It is best to evaluate the complete picture as it fits your particular lifestyle when selecting an RV home base state.

It is not a good idea to use one state for mail forwarding, another for a driver's license, another as a legal address for tax filing, etc. States might think you are attempting to avoid paying their taxes or fees.

Chapter 4 How Should I Plan?

We got some good advice when we started out full-timing about planning. You're beginning a journey such as you have never done before. The best way to approach this journey is with sound planning. You don't want to come off the road and have regrets that you haven't done the things you wanted to do.

Goals

The first and most important part of the planning process is to set goals for both yourself and your partner. Will you stay in RV resorts and tour the country, or will you move with the seasons (snow birding), or will you see every major league ballpark? Would you like to tour Civil War battlefields? You must have goals, or you will meander aimlessly; or perhaps that is your goal. You can have multiple goals; just remember how long you might be at this. It would be gratifying to accomplish your main goals and then talk about the stuff you did with friends and family. You might even convince someone else to try the full-time lifestyle.

Short Term Goals

Short term goals are the things you want to accomplish within the next year. This way, you can be specific and even lay out a tentative route. This is actually the most difficult type of planning because you will start executing the short term plan immediately. Better get it right before the meandering starts. This type of planning works hand in hand with the budgeting process. You need to know you can afford to do the things you have planned for the year ahead of you.

An example of a short term plan might be to visit all the state and national parks in several states. Another could be to attend a number of rallies across the country. Whatever you plan, try to keep it realistic. A business term I used to use is "don't boil the ocean". In other words, don't plan so much you couldn't possibly do it all in a year. Kathy and I only had one destination we had to do the first year, and that was to see Mount Rushmore. We did that and so much more.

If you are over fifty years old like we are, you must plan on visiting your doctor once a year to get physical exams and renew prescriptions. We have forgotten this and consequently we have doctors in three states.

Trip Planning

Trip planning, short term goals and budgeting all work together. Once you set the goals, you are in a position to start planning the trip. Kathy and I do the goal setting together and then I do the rough trip planning. I get out the maps, the campground guides, and the planning software and lay out a route that takes us either directly to our destinations or near enough to visit by car. We make sure we will have the funds to do what is in the plan, or we revise the plan.

Midterm Goals

A good midterm plan might reach out five years or so. There are over four hundred National Parks in the continental U.S. You could realistically expect to thoroughly tour about a hundred and fifty or so in five years assuming you won't do much else. You could, however, visit forty-nine states and spend a month or so in each. If you snowbird from warm weather to warm weather, the midterm planning is easy. If you want to tour the country, seasons play a large part in the planning process.

Kathy and I continue to visit as many National Parks as we can when our route takes us near one. Of course we also do National Monuments, and there are a ton of those. Our main focus is to find new and interesting places to explore and share our experiences on our radio show.

Long Term Goals

Long term goals encompass your total full-time RVing experience. This could go out ten or twenty years or more. This is where you can do a little "blue sky" planning, commonly known as dreaming. Once you have it down on paper, figure out how you can make it happen. You might want to get another rig sometime in the future. Put it in the plan; you can always revise it later on. It is a fact that we all age more quickly in our later years. I hate trying to do stuff I love but just can't do anymore. You might want to make allowance for that.

Exit Plan

We are planning at least another ten years on the road as long as our health allows; but we are setting up a plan for being off the road.

Someday it will be time to hang up the keys and either have a stick built house again, or park the RV and stay. Many of you who are reading this are thinking WOW, I haven't even started and you want me to think about stopping. No way! Yes, way!! Planning ahead is very important. Nothing you decide today is written in stone, but you should have an idea of what you will do. These plans will change and evolve. It's up to you, but it is something to think about.

Where will you hang up the keys? Will it be close to the kids, or maybe there's a mountain lake or a seaside resort that you really like. You may not have found it yet, but as you travel, keep your eyes open to any possibility. Maybe there's a city you have fallen in love with or an RV park where great friends have been made and you want to spend time with them.

Things to consider are weather, medical facilities, proximity to a city, and of course, is there a WalMart or commissary close by. Is there a church you like? How much will it cost to stay in this area? If it is an RV Park, are you a co-owner or will the rent or fees be going up every year? Does the park have a reserve fund for major repairs, or will there be an assessment fee? Who actually runs the park, a manager or a board of directors? What are the rules? Can you build a casita, and how big? Can water and sewer be added to the shed? How about when you decide to sell, will you get your investment back or does that really matter to you?

A lot of snowbirds just love the winter time to be with friends and play cards, golf, play dominos, practice line dancing and they eventually buy a park model trailer and stay the whole year. Maybe a stick built house is what you will want. Where will you settle? Will you buy one and rent it out or live in it part time. Maybe you can afford to have several. What will you do if one of you becomes seriously ill or passes away? I believe in the Boy Scout motto "be prepared". If you have a plan, then at the time of the emergency you will know what to do because you have already made decisions. The decision doesn't have to be made today, but it will need to be made at some point in time.

Chapter 5 What About Your Stuff?

You have decided to go full-timing and now it's time to sell the house. Whether you choose a realtor or do it yourself, get ready. This is not a quick process. You will want the best price for your house, so consult someone who will help you decide what needs painting and/or repair. Think about the price you would consider, and what bottom line price you will accept for the house.

One of the first things to understand is that almost everything you own is "stuff". It can be replaced. What cannot be replaced, such as family pictures and artwork, can either be put in storage or on loan to your family. We started by calling our children and telling them to bring a U-Haul and take anything they wanted. After they did and we had taken out the few things that we considered non-replaceable, we scheduled 2 yard sales. This does take some time; you can usually get a yard sale kit from the local newspaper that will help you with the process. The most important thing to remember is that you are trying to get rid of everything, and price it accordingly. After the sale we contacted the Salvation Army to come and pick up anything that was left. This can be kind of hard to do, but there is only so much space in the RV for things that will be important. Choose wisely.

If there are some things that you cannot get rid of, find a storage unit and rent it for a year. After that year go through all of this again and make a decision. We have friends that had 3 storage units and they returned every year trying to cut down what they had stored. Finally, after about 5 years they were able to get rid of everything that they didn't need. Paying for storage units can be expensive, so really think about what you want to store. We made the decision to go the whole way and just sold everything we could.

You may also want to consider donating to your local church or charity. They will greatly appreciate whatever you can give.

Do you have two cars? One must go. Since we bought a motor home, we knew we would be towing and we choose the newer car. We took our second car back to the dealership and they gave us a great price for it and that took care of that. We also had to modify the car with a transmission pump to make it towable with all four wheels down. This decision was made because the car was already paid off and to buy a new towable car would cost a lot more money than the modification. Only you can decide what you want to do. Again choose wisely. The more money you have available to tour with will make your full-timing life more enjoyable.

Chapter 6 Do you have Health Care Insurance?

In the seven plus years Kathy and I have been on the road, she has had two surgeries and I have had one. I was hospitalized for four days in Florida with a still unknown virus. If we had not possessed good health insurance, our life on the road would have been over. I am retired from the U.S. Navy and have the good fortune to have excellent health insurance for both of us. Now we are both on Medicare and the military insurance pays all costs Medicare doesn't. This is probably the best situation to be in. Many of you will have health insurance from a previous employer or from your state in some cases. That's great!

We have talked to fellow full-timers who have medical insurance from a previous employment that is only in effect if they are in the original state of that employment. Apparently there are supplemental policies for out of state travel, but the cost is high.

Affordability is in the eye of the beholder, but there are many companies that will provide varying levels of health insurance for a monthly or semi-annual fee. The obvious point here is even a short hospitalization can produce tens of thousands of dollars in costs and an office or urgent care visit with the attending tests can run into several thousands. If you set out on the full-time lifestyle without health insurance, you are betting everything you have that neither of you will become seriously ill. It's a crapshoot my friends. I cannot in good conscience recommend this lifestyle to you without you having adequate health insurance coverage.

This is a good time to mention medications. We have a mail order prescription service called Express Scripts. We give them a delivery address as we travel and get most of our meds that way. Some of our refillable prescriptions are through WalMart and Good Sam Club pharmacies. Just show the packaging or the prescription number to the local store and you can get your meds that way. We use WalMart primarily because they are found almost anywhere in the country. We asked our doctor to set us up with 1 year prescriptions in ninety day packages. This way we can plan in advance when we may be running low. No matter who you choose, make sure they have outlets where you will be travelling.

Chapter 7 How Am I Going to Pay for This?

No matter how you live the RV lifestyle, you will need money on a regular basis to continue to enjoy it. This isn't much fun to deal with, but it must be done to ensure you are able to continue this lifestyle. You have to decide how much you are willing to spend in order to maintain whatever level of RV lifestyle you desire. We have talked to folks that said they had to spend over five thousand dollars a month to be happy. Wow! We have discussed this issue with others that boon-dock in one place for long periods that can do it on as little as several hundred dollars a month. We fall in between someplace.

There are numerous variables that have to be considered to come to a reliable figure for you. To start off, you need to determine all your fixed monthly costs such as insurance, rig and car payments, phone, internet, television, and other communications expenses, and any others you may have. See the budget section for more ideas. Now we'll add in the variable expenses. You must decide on your basic lifestyle. Will you eat out in restaurants, or will you make most of your meals, or something in between? Will you boondock, or live off the grid, or will you stay in campgrounds and resorts? Will you travel a certain range of miles every month, or will you stay put for a season? Will you work while out on the road, and if so how much money do you expect to make? Most workamping jobs pay minimum wage, so be realistic. These and many other questions must be answered in order to come to a realistic dollar figure.

Once you have arrived at a monthly income requirement, subtract that from the total of your actual available income. Anything that is a positive number is great and can be put into savings. If you have a negative total, then you must reconsider your lifestyle desires. You may have to work to supplement income, or travel less to reduce fuel expense, or make other accommodations. In our case, workamping has brought us lifelong friends and some wonderful experiences. Check out our working on the road section for more information.

Chapter 8 Do You Have a Budget?

Here are the nuts and bolts of budgeting for the RV lifestyle. Most of this applies equally to full-time and part-time RVing.

Fixed Costs

Fixed costs are those that recur on a regular basis either annually, quarterly, or monthly. These are the must-pay items that you can't change easily.

The RV

If you do not pay cash for your RV this will be your biggest recurring expense. Whether you choose a class A, B, or C motor home, 5th wheel, travel trailer or pop-up, you will have payments to make. We choose a Class A diesel motor home and to tow a small car. The best advice we have heard is to buy the RV you would have probably bought after the first two first. Full-timing is hard on a rig and try and buy the very best you can comfortably afford.

Towed or Towing Vehicle

If you have a motor home you will probably need a towed vehicle. It is easy to park the rig and hop in the car and off you go for another adventure. Be sure and find out if the car is flat towable, that means 4 wheels down. You can modify your tow like we did because our car was paid for and it was less expensive to modify the car than buy a new one. If you want to travel in a 5th wheel or travel trailer, you will need a tow vehicle. Make sure you check the towing specifications for your tow vehicle and match it to the weights of your trailer.

Vehicle Insurance

By registering in a less populated state, your insurance costs can be lower. We were in Florida when we first bought our rig, but decided on South Dakota as out state of domicile. Not many people live in South Dakota and our auto and motor home insurance cost went down by a third. Your car and RV will both need to be covered and not all insurance companies will cover for full time use of the RV. Be honest when you fill out the application. The insurance company could cancel your coverage or deny a claim if they discover you were untruthful on the application.

Extended Warranty

Since we bought a used motor home, we also carry Extended Warranty and it has paid for its cost several times. A towing service is also quite important. We use Coach-Net and they have been great. The first question they ask when we call is always "are you in a safe place". That is a great comfort and peace of mind.

Vehicle Registration

Every year your car or truck and rig will need to be registered. Don't forget to plan for this expense.

Health Insurance

Health insurance is a key to being able to enjoy the full-time RV lifestyle. If you don't have coverage from prior employment or Medicare, it is available for purchase from many companies. Make sure your healthcare is available across the country. Some plans are only good in the original state of purchase.

Communication

Cell phones and internet are so important to keep in contact with family and friends. We have Verizon cell service and its air card for internet. Anymore it is hard to find a pay phone and almost everyone has a cell phone. Most campgrounds will have some form of WI-FI; however it is not always good. Some use Tengo internet which is a service available in most states at a cost. Almost all public libraries have free internet service and many fast food places offer it free. Just remember that public Wi-Fi is not secure. I would never do my banking or post credit card information using public Wi-Fi.

Television

Some parks have cable TV and will charge extra (up to $3.00 a day) for its use. We use Direct TV satellite service and we like it very much. The monthly bill is paid online. If you will be in a park for an extended period and the park has cable services, most satellite TV companies will allow you to put the service to "sleep" for six months.

Mail Forwarding Service

How do I get my mail? This is the first question we hear. You will need to get a mail forwarding service which will assign you an address at their office. All of your mail will be sent to this address and then they will forward it to you. There are several companies that provide this service and are listed in the "How Do You Get Your Mail" section. They usually charge a yearly fee and then you will pay the postage to forward the mail to wherever you are located. We have cut way back on our mail. Getting rid of flyers and magazines we do not read cuts the weight of the shipped mail. We do everything we can by internet. Many magazines are available in an on-line version, and generally at a lower cost than the newsstand version.

Variable or Controllable Costs

Variable expenses are those that you have some control over. This is the first place to look when you need to cut back.

Fuel

Fuel is probably the biggest variable expense that you will have. So, consider your travel distance and the average price for fuel where you are traveling; add a few cents to the calculation of the expense and travel accordingly. We plan out 2-3 months in advance and figure out the miles and the cost. To find out how much it will cost for fuel in the different states you will be traveling thru, go on the internet and look at the Pilot/Flying J http://www.pilotflyingj.com/ or Loves http://www.loves.com/ websites. They list the current prices for fuel on a daily bases at all of their stations. There can be as much as ten cents per gallon or more difference between one state and another. Plan your trip based on these variable expenses. Sometimes we stay longer, and sometimes we will do fewer miles. There is no rush to get anywhere, so just enjoy the place you are now for a few more weeks. Don't forget the liquid propane (LP) tank. We use liquid propane for heating water, the stove top, and the furnaces in cold weather, and the refrigerator if needed. With the motor home's built-in propane tank, we fill up wherever we find the best price; but except for colder winters, it is usually only two or three times a year. Most of our propane use is for the stove. Because we tend to grill a lot, we have a small LP tank just for the barbeque grill.

Camping

Parks range in price from zero dollars to over one hundred dollars a night and more. It all depends on the kind of park you like to stay in. Boon docking (camping without hook-ups) is using the self-contained features of your RV such as water holding tanks, generator or solar panels for electricity, etc. Boon docking is great fun. We have done it several times and enjoyed it. We don't do a lot, but there are those who will park for months at a time with no camping fees. Staying longer at the campground will give you a better price, and you will have more time to explore the area.

Some campers think it is okay to stay at WalMart or other store parking lots for free for an extended period of time. Please don't do this. It isn't fair to the store or the local campgrounds.

Belonging to a camping club like Escapees, Good Sam, FMCA, Thousand Trails, RPI or Passport America will give you a discount of some type; usually between ten and fifty percent. We have used them all.

Passport America advertises itself as half-price camping and is more cost effective, but there are restrictions to the length of stay and the time of year. You need to read the fine print.

Camping Clubs like Thousand Trails, Outdoor World, AOR, Western Horizons, and Coast to Coast have an initial cost that can be high, then there is an annual fee, but the only extras you have to pay for would be for fifty amp electrical service. A new program at Thousand Trails is the Zone Pass that allows free camping for 30 nights and $3 per night thereafter for $500 in one of four geographical zones. All of these clubs can be found online for resale. Be sure to check it out.

Then there are the individual private membership parks that are affiliated with the big clubs. There are many throughout the US. We have been able to camp in many of them to check them out thru our Resort Parks International (RPI) membership. These are great for a home park near the grandkids or to visit each year for your annual check-up. Again, there is an annual maintenance fee. Also check out if there are reserve funds for any major repairs. You don't want to have a huge unexpected assessment fee.

National and State Parks are a great option. They are beautiful and not too expensive. The only thing we have found is that the do not always accommodate larger rigs. Again, call or go on the internet to check out the restrictions.

The Escapees RV Club has nineteen parks in their system for the use of club members at rates below twenty dollars per night.

Food

It is your choice whether you eat out a lot or cook in your rig. This is a major expense that you have control over. We have changed towards eating at home and only going out once every 2 weeks. We do a lot of barbequing and grilling, many times we will cook two meals at a time, so lunch or dinner is all ready for the following day. It's good to have a nice grill and a portable LP tank, this will help keep the heat out of the rig during those long summer days, and there is nothing finer than a hamburger grilled outside. There are grocery stores everywhere and something is always on sale. We have found planning out meals for a week at a time and taking a list to the store saves a lot of money as well as clipping coupons.

Maintenance and Repair

Just like your stick built house there are regular maintenance and repairs that will need to be done. Getting these done and keeping a record will help to prevent major breakdowns in the future. About every five to seven years you will need new tires on the motor home. 5th wheels and travel trailers seem to need tires a lot. If you have a diesel engine the yearly oil change and lube can cost as much as $500.00. This is a big expense; plan to put aside a small amount monthly so you are ready. Consider buying an extended warranty (such as Good Sam Extended Warranty); we have this, and it has come in handy several times.

Laundry

If you do not have a washer in the rig, this is another expense. It runs about $10 to $15 a week depending on how much the campground or Laundromat is charging.

Banking

We do all of our banking on the internet. Most banks and credit unions have websites for on-line banking. Bills and payments are scheduled and controlled through this system. Some banks have new plans for depositing checks into your account using an iPad or iPhone. Let your bank know that you will be full timing so they will not be alarmed by charges from all over the country. However, it is your job to check your accounts constantly and keep track of the charges. We have had no problems as of yet. Be careful of public Wi-Fi hotspots for internet connection when banking. These sites are not secure and you don't want your information to be made public. See the "How Will You Communicate?" section.

These are just some of the examples of the expenses you will have. You may have credit card and car payments to handle. If possible try to pay off everything leaving the most important and lowest interest debt for last. Carrying heavy debt can make RVing a nightmare. Be wise and realistic in your finances. Always figure on the high side and you will not run short.

As with everything we have talked about, do your research and talk with others. Talk to your bank or credit union, phone service, TV service and take names for later reference. If possible, get written confirmation of issues you have discussed.

Chapter 9 How Will You Get Your Mail?

This is almost always the first question we get when we talk about full timing with people. To be honest, I would be happy to never get any mail. It becomes clutter, and we already have enough of that. But, until electronic means make it obsolete, we must still deal with mail. A lot of folks we know have their adult children take care of sending their mail to them. This is fine, but they are busy and sometimes the mail is a low priority for them. It's a hassle to package it and go to the post office, send it, and pay the postage.

When we started on the road from Florida, we used a Mailboxes, Etc., http://www.mbe.com/ for forwarding our First Class mail. This worked out fairly well, but there were problems with "junk" mail and the service was comparatively expensive. Since that time, we are convinced that dedicated mail forwarding services are the best solution to getting your mail on the road. A recent Google check of "mail forwarding" yielded more than 80 actual mail forwarding services. We were in the process of changing our state of domicile to South Dakota, so we decided to use a service in that state. We ended up with a company called Alternative Resources, one of the more popular mail forwarders from South Dakota. Most of these mail services work in a similar fashion. There is a monthly or annual fee for the service, and then a deposit of fifty to a hundred dollars for postage charged to a credit card, replenished when the postage account falls to a pre-determined low point. Like most of the larger services, they were quite flexible with what class of mail we wanted forwarded and what method such as First Class, or Priority Mail, or even Federal Express or United Parcel Service. They were also flexible with how many shipments we would receive. We could have it shipped weekly, bi-weekly, monthly, or a one-time shipment when we were traveling.

One important thing to remember is that unless you are a seasonal resident, most campgrounds will not receive mail for you; they just don't have the staff, nor do they want to get into difficulties with the United States Postal Service. We use the General Delivery service at local Post Offices in the area where we are camped. Be careful in this as certain Post Offices will not handle General Delivery mail. Get the zip code of the campground where you will be staying and call the Post Office. Verify that they will handle

General Delivery and also the zip code and address of that Post Office. This may seem like a hassle, but so is chasing a missed delivery with time sensitive material in it.

Of all the mail services we have looked into, the Escapees RV Club mail service is a world class operation. Located in Livingston, TX, it has its own zip code. You must be a member of the Escapees RV Club to use their mail service, however. Go to http://www.escapees.com/ .

Next up is Alternative Resources, located in Sioux Falls, South Dakota. This is our choice as it is in our new home state. Go to www.alternativeresources.net . Other South Dakota mail forwarders are www.mydakotaaddress.com in Madison, South Dakota and America's Mailbox in Box Elder, South Dakota at www.americas-mailbox.com . There are others available in South Dakota; you just have to search the web for South Dakota mail forwarding.

If you want to have your official domicile in Florida, the Good Sam Club operates a mail service from Pensacola, Florida. Go to http://www.goodsammail.com/. Another mail service located in Crestview, Florida is http://www.myrvmail.com/. Again, there are other mail forwarding services in Florida, just look them up on the web.

Based in Cincinnati, Ohio, the Family Motor Coach Association runs a mail service for their members. Check out http://www.fmca.com/ .

There are mail services based in many other states, I have only highlighted the major ones in the states most frequently used by full time RVers. Spend some time searching the internet to find the ideal service to fit your needs. You should also check out RV forums such as the one on http://www.rv.net/ for plusses and minuses before settling on this important part of the full time lifestyle.

Chapter 10 How Will You Communicate?

Since we are full-timers and not weekend campers, we need to stay in touch with our families, friends, business and banking interests. All I can say is, "Thank God for cellular communications and the World Wide Web!" I'm not sure how this absolute dependence on fast communications developed, but we are addicts. When we can't get cell phone service, we are almost lost and devastated. Something might happen and we won't know it within three minutes. OMG!! Sorry, I got carried away a little. It is true, however, that we desire the fastest and most reliable access to communications media. So then, how will we do this?

Cellular Telephone Service on the Road

In my opinion, this is a primary need. We use cell phones to contact emergency services either by dialing 911, or to call a towing and/or repair service after a breakdown. A motor home with a towed car doubles the chance that you might need to call for assistance. Of course, we also desire to talk with our family members and friends for birthdays, anniversaries, and just to chat. Occasionally we use the phone to contact our bank, credit union, and Credit Card Company if problems develop. I could go on, but you get the point. We need cellular coverage.

Most cellular communication in use today is 3G or Third Generation. This refers to the technology used to move calls along a long string of cell towers. Lately, 4G or fourth generation technology is becoming more prevalent in the more densely populated cities. This is a much faster service and is capable of streaming video content without slowing down, depending on the area and high or low usage. Hopefully, 4G will roll out to the more rural locations soon.

Three companies are the most popular among full time RVers. They are AT&T, Sprint, and Verizon. At the time of this writing, AT&T is stronger in the cities and Verizon has the best coverage nationwide. Sprint is gaining and may soon be equal to the others. All three have available electronic bill paying via the internet. We prefer that to getting bills sent through the mail and possibly arriving late.

What happens when you don't have a strong enough cellular signal to make and receive calls? I'm glad you asked. Enter the cell phone amplifier. The purpose of a cell phone amplifier is to boost the signal it receives from its own antenna and feed that signal into your cell phone with a cable. That is fine as long as your phone has an external antenna jack, which many don't. What to do? Enter the wireless cell phone amplifier. Now the amplifier has both an exterior antenna to communicate with the cell tower and an interior antenna to communicate with the cell phone. We use a cellular amplifier and antennas from Wilson Electronics, the biggest and most well-known supplier of this type of equipment. Go to www.wilsonelectronics.com . This technology works great if you are in a fringe area, or have buildings or hills between you and the cell tower. Unfortunately, there are areas in our country without cellular service of any kind. We have been in a few of these areas. The only thing to do is drive until you get to an area with enough signal strength to make calls. These areas are mostly in the unpopulated areas of the western states. Check the map of your cell phone provider to find these "dead zones".

Over the last several years, "Smart Phones" have been introduced. These are cellular telephones that can be connected to the internet and are GPS enabled, so they know where they are. Besides having internet access, the coolest thing about smart phones is applications. You must have heard the current catch phrase "There's an app for that". Applications are mini programs that accomplish a specific function and run on smart phones and tablet devices. This technology started with the Apple iPhone and iPad and quickly migrated to other manufacturer's operating systems such as Android and Blackberry. It's hard to believe, but there are hundreds of thousands of applications such as games, finance and banking, business, navigation, and so many more. A search using the letters "RV" in the Apple App Store returned more than 250 different apps. It's a little overwhelming, but we have settled on a few app's we use a lot. "Allstays RV" is an application that uses GPS and your current location to find campgrounds along the way with descriptions, contact information, and even reviews. "Gas Buddy" gives the current fuel prices at either stations near you, or at a location you select. We use two weather apps frequently. One is "The Weather Channel" for current weather and forecasts. The other is called "Radar Now". This one gives us the weather radar picture of our location using GPS. A lot of these apps are free, and most are less than ten dollars. New apps are being introduced constantly for all the various platforms. We make driving decisions based on the weather apps.

Connecting to the Internet

Next to a working cell phone, internet access has the highest priority among the communications mediums. There are several ways to get on the internet, including a telephone modem providing high speed DSL, or dial-up services if available at a campground, Wi-Fi, data communication via cellular technology, and satellite connection.

Dial up

Dial-up internet service can be available at your campsite if there is an active phone connection available. Connected through the telephone jack installed in most later model RVs or at a connection jack in the clubhouse, this is the slowest and least reliable method of internet connection. High speed internet via a Digital Subscriber Line (DSL) modem can provide fast internet speeds, but usually requires at least a three to six month local service contract commitment.

WI-FI

According to the internet encyclopedia Wikipedia, Wi-Fi is a popular technology that allows an electronic device to exchange data wirelessly using radio waves over a computer network, including high-speed internet connections. Currently, this is probably the most popular method to connect to the internet. It is used by laptop and desktop computers, new technology smart phones, tablet devices such as the Apple iPad, and others. Wi-Fi adapters of various capabilities have been standard in laptop computers for several years. The speed of the connection is dependent on many variables, including the strength of the received and transmitted radio signal, the capability of the installed Wi-Fi adapter, obstructions such as trees and buildings in the line of sight between antenna and computer, and the bandwidth of the park's connection to the internet. It is possible to have a five bar signal at the computer, but slow or no service due to too many users on a less than capable system. This happens frequently at larger parks. At first, campground Wi-Fi was free, but more and more campgrounds and resorts are installing pay-as-you go systems. This does not guarantee fast uninterrupted service, however. A second possible problem with Wi-Fi is that it is not secure. Many things have been tried, but public Wi-Fi is not secure, and you want to do your banking on-line. Enough said.

Cellular Data Connection

This is the method Kathy and I use to access the internet. The simplest way is to have a Smart Phone such as an Apple iPhone, or an Android smart phone. These are capable of internet connection and retrieving e-mail. Small screen and limited battery life are concerns. Lately the introduction of the Apple iPad and other tablet devices has overcome the small screen and battery life issues. Kathy can get by with nothing but her iPad for all her internet use. Of course, being a techie, I need more. It is possible to tether a data capable cellular phone to a laptop computer with the addition of some inexpensive software. This could be great if you have a cell phone with an unlimited data account. Those account features are going the way of dinosaurs. The next possibility is an air card, which is essentially a cellular phone optimized for data. This requires a separate plan from your cellular phone provider of between fifty and eighty dollars a month, depending on bandwidth, or how much data you will receive from and transmit to the internet. It is a small device that connects to a computer's USB port. With the proper software and activation codes, you will be able to have high speed internet access whenever you have a cell signal. There are other similar devices available that can simultaneously connect up to five devices such as computers, tablets, and wireless printers to the internet.

We have added a wireless router to our home network. This device will accept either an air card or a Wi-Fi signal and transmit it with an onboard radio. This is similar to your own Wi-Fi hotspot, but with a hardware firewall to provide security for your data. It can handle many more devices than I will ever own. When there is no cellular signal, it will default to the strongest Wi-Fi signal available.

Now that we have added a wireless cellular amplifier to our arsenal of communication devices, we have both a cell phone "cloud" within our rig and a secure Wi-Fi cloud as well.

Satellite Connection to the Internet

Prior to cellular internet connection, satellite internet systems were the best and most reliable way to connect to the internet. Hughes

Corporation, which provides internet connectivity by way of the HughesNet Company, operates a constellation of communications satellites accessed by dish antennas mounted on houses and other structures. The Datastorm Company has made this technology portable. They provide a roof mounted collapsible dish with automated raising and pointing electronics for motor home or trailer use. The system costs around five thousand dollars and installation can add another thousand. Monthly service fees start at about sixty dollars a month. This works great in Alaska and Mexico where cell service is spotty to non-existent. Unfortunately, internet signal speeds at best are slower than cellular internet for the same monthly rate. Another drawback is that the bandwidth on the particular satellite you are subscribed to may be oversold. This means that when many users are online, the speed can drop as low as dial-up slow. There is a tripod mounted satellite dish available for around fifteen hundred dollars, but the monthly fees are the same and the same speed roadblocks apply. Unless you are stuck in an area with no cell service, I cannot in good conscience recommend this type of system when cellular internet is so easy and affordable.

Television

I have included television because it is a form of one-way communication. We love to watch TV, but having The Weather Channel can be a necessity during severe weather. It must be important because almost every RV we see has a crank-up "Bat wing" antenna installed. We have one, and we use it wherever we have adequate local channels available. These antennas are also capable of receiving High Definition (HD) signals if you have a newer television set with an HD receiver.

If you absolutely "must" have TV, satellite reception is the answer. Satellite service is available from Direct TV or from Dish Network. We have had both and I see little difference in either content of service. Customer service can be difficult because most of the agents do not understand the fact that our antennas move around, but eventually you will convince them. There are many packages of satellite service you can order with increasing monthly subscription costs.

If you have a roof mounted dome satellite antenna, bear in mind that if you desire HD programming, you are limited to Dish

Network. Direct TV HD broadcasts require the acquisition of at least three satellite feeds. Consequently, a larger antenna than what will fit in a dome is needed. Also remember that your dome could be blocked by trees in your campsite.

Our rig came with a crank-up satellite dish. We used it for five years with our Direct TV subscription. At the same time, we had another dish we used on a tripod when we were parked where trees would block the satellite signal. Now we have upgraded to an HD TV so we needed an HD compatible dish. It is larger and heavier than the standard dish. We had to find a heavy duty tripod for it, but it works well and we are quite pleased with it. I recommend a website that I found when searching for the tripod. Go to http://www.tv4rv.com . They have a monthly newsletter with plenty of valuable advice for setting up and pointing satellite dishes.

Chapter 11 How do I Get Good Information on RVs?

Homework is going to RV shows, dealerships, and RV club rallies as well as talking with a number of full-timers to get various insights. Visiting a dealership can be good if you make it quite clear to the inevitable salesman assigned to you that you are in the investigating stage and are absolutely not ready to make a purchase. Always take a small notebook and a camera with you when looking at RVs. By the time you have climbed into twenty or thirty rigs, they all tend to run together. Write down the model and what features you like and which ones you don't. Make a note of the MSRP (Manufacturer's Suggested Retail Price), but don't let that sway you. RV buying is a negotiation and MSRP is relatively useless as anything but a starting point, especially with used rigs.

When Kathy and I look at rigs, I start with a walk around and look into all basement doors. This way I get a feel for how much storage is available, how easy it is to access engine filters, batteries, fuse panels, and other service items. This is also when I make a note of the age of the tires using the DOT code on the tire. If the rig is used and you are interested in it, go up on the roof and check out the conditions up there. Are there cracks in the caulking, tears in membrane material, black mildew? Are there loose items that will rattle and make noise at 55 miles per hour? These are issues that must be addressed prior to purchase.

Kathy goes inside and will pretend to do routine household chores like cooking a meal, changing a bed, and other things we do on a regular basis. Is there enough counter space? One of her hot buttons is whether there is enough pantry space for food and supplies close to the cooking area. Is there adequate room around the bed to move easily? Is the dinette comfortable for eating? If the rig is motorized, I check out the cockpit for easy access to all driver controls, comfort of the driver's seat for long hours on the road, and other amenities. All this goes into the notebook.

After a while, you will get a feel for what things are important and you might make up a check-list for evaluating an RV for possible purchase. I would resist the temptation to take a test drive at this point in the homework. You don't want the salesman to salivate and count his commission in advance, do you? Save that for when you have settled on a few models that you are interested in making a purchase decision on. You might consider getting the DVD "Buying a Recreational Vehicle" from the Better Business Bureau. It is available from The RV Bookstore

We do these same things when we look at rigs at RV shows and large rallies with RV displays. One thing to remember, today's "Show Special" will be just as special, and just as good a deal next week or even next month. At most shows and rallies, you will receive a plastic bag at the entrance with some brochures and show info. Stuff this bag with brochures on all the rigs you think might be a possibility for future purchase. This gives you valuable information for comparison of different rigs. You might even consider a backpack for carrying these and your notebook and camera. If a price is listed on a rig, write that on the brochure.

I wish we would have had a small voice recorder when we talked to other experienced RVers. We spent over an hour with two full-timer couples at the Escapees RV Club booth at the Tampa, Florida Super Show talking about the full-time lifestyle. That conversation was a confirmation that full-time RVing was what we wanted to do. This was a year before we bought our rig. We still had a lot of homework to do even though we knew this was to be our future.

Chapter 12 What Kind of RV Will You Live In?

Choosing your RV can be a lot of fun if you approach it with a plan you both agree on. We have met folks who are camping seasonally in a short 25 foot travel trailer. Others have to have the largest rig available. You both have to agree on the lifestyle you want to live. Some folks are into ATVs and other motorized "toys" and a good fit for them would be a toy hauler. Maybe you want to travel around our beautiful country and see as much of it as possible? Others may want to settle in for a season and move with the changing seasons. Can you say "Snowbird"? While there is no ideal rig for a particular lifestyle, the decision is up to you. Unless you can figure out how to live full-time in a class B conversion van, you will probably need to tow something. You might tow a fifth wheel trailer behind a truck or tow a car or truck behind a motor home, but you will most likely be towing. This, too, factors into the decision of what RV to buy. In order to avoid a major financial mistake, make sure the rig you choose is the right unit for the lifestyle you have chosen. You won't know the magnitude of your mistake until you go to trade the rig in.

When we were in the homework phase of deciding what rig to buy, we got a lot of advice, sometimes conflicting, about whether to buy a new or a pre-owned rig. We'll look at both sides of the issue. A new rig of any type will have warranties on the chassis, drive train for motorized units, and appliances such as refrigerators, air conditioners, stove and hot water heater and furnace(s). This is great peace of mind for many folks. Another issue is that you will be the first to use the unit so everything will be pristine. There won't be bedbugs in the mattress or stains on the carpet. Obviously, this is appealing to many people. The big ugly cloud over any RV purchase is depreciation. No RV will increase in value. Drive off depreciation on any new rig will be at least twenty percent. On the more expensive units, it will be more. As each year passes, the depreciation continues in smaller increments. To quote from Bob Randall; Mark Polk (2011-09-29). RV Buyers Survival Guide (Kindle Locations 684-685). RV Education 101. Kindle Edition. "Depreciation is only a major problem if you pay full MSRP (Manufacturer's Suggested Retail). Depreciation is figured based on what the unit should have sold for, not what you paid for it." We bought this book prior to our RV purchase; it should be an essential part of every future RV purchase you make.

A maddening problem is that almost all new rigs have "issues". These can be drawers that don't fit properly, appliances that don't work as they should, small leaks around windows and roof mounted items, and other such annoying things that fall under the warranty. Axel misalignment is a common issue with towable RVs that manifests itself with premature tire wear and even blow-outs. Even though covered, the RV must be returned to the dealer for service and repairs, thus robbing you of the use of your rig. In extreme cases, this can go on and on for months. Even the most thorough pre-delivery inspection can miss some things.

A two to three year old RV will have had most if not all of those "new rig bugs" fixed and/or resolved. The first two or three years are the largest chunk of depreciation as well. A two to three year old motor home will probably have some warranty left on the drive train. We spent a lot of time doing the math and we calculated cost of a new motor home to still be more expensive versus a two year old unit with better specifications. At the end of the day, we decided on a one year old rig with much more equipment than what we were originally considering. This fell right in line with another bit of advice we had heard which was, "Buy your third rig first". An entry level unit will have a more acceptable price, but you will probably be looking for a better one in a year or two. Now you will have two sets of depreciation to deal with as well as sales commissions. We have heard of folks buying three or four RVs within five years. What an expensive hassle! On the other hand, unless you and/or your partner are experienced handymen, buying a fifteen year old rig might end up being more expensive than a five year old one.

This whole decision process is both subjective and emotional. Debates rage over motor home or fifth wheel trailer. Another constant question is gasoline power versus diesel. New versus used is always a lively discussion. There is no right answer. You must decide what will work best for you. We will give our opinions about these and other issues, but they are *our* opinions based on what we thought we would need and what we could afford. We also will look at rigs that easily lend themselves to full time RVing. I'm sure there must be full-timers living in truck campers, pop-up tent campers, and teardrop trailers, but I'm not going to spend any time on those rigs.

When we were looking at motor homes and fifth wheel trailers, a friend described the following word picture. You are in your motor home traveling with another RVer in a fifth wheel trailer. You're running late and arrive at the campground just as darkness falls. As you are pulling in to your pull-thru campsite, the rain starts falling in sheets. Am I graphic enough? Your job in your motor home is to put your jacks down to level the coach, open up whatever slide rooms are necessary, shut down the motor and go to bed. You can hook up power, water and sewer in the morning. Your buddy is going to get very wet before he can rest his weary head. He has to get out of his nice warm and dry truck and put down four corner jacks. If he is extremely lucky, they will be electric. This is common in only the high-end trailers. Then he can go inside the trailer and extend whatever slide rooms are needed to move around inside and try to dry off. "I'm just sayin'."

Class "A" Motor Home

The Class "A" is the top of the food chain for RVs. They cost more, they're bigger than other RVs and they are just macho cool. The amenities in a class "A" make it a condo on wheels. Multiple large screen televisions with surround sound systems are common. Combination washer/dryers are available as well as a separate stacked washer and dryer. Electric residential refrigerators are available on many newer coaches. Almost all have combination convection and microwave ovens. Slide-out rooms provide more square footage for living aboard. Built-in central vacuum systems are common options. How about an electric fireplace under that large flat-screen? Basement storage is an advantage common to both gas and diesel motor homes. There are doors along both sides that open into storage compartments to hold gear you don't need inside the coach. Depending on the chassis, there may be pass-thru storage accessible from either side. Almost all class "A" coaches will have either hydraulic or electric jacks for leveling the coach.

OK, I'll start at the top. The Class "A" diesel pusher motor home was our choice almost eight years ago, and we haven't changed our minds. A key point is lots of storage and basement space. We have almost four thousand pounds of available cargo carrying capacity. That's a lot of grills and lawn chairs. The diesel chassis provides air brakes and air bag assisted suspension. This makes for both safe and comfortable driving. A side benefit to this is an air chuck tied to the on-board air compressor for airing up tires. It also has the ability to handle four slide-out rooms. I've even seen five on one rig. I was told by the tour guide at the Winnebago plant that each slide room can add as much as one thousand pounds of extra weight to the coach. That big motor provides plenty of torque to move all that weight up hills. An exhaust brake or a mechanical engine retarder is provided to help save the service brakes going down those same hills. Another benefit with the engine in the back is very low noise when driving, although there are some front engine diesel entry level motor homes on the market today. Typically, a diesel coach will get a little better mileage than a gasoline engine Class "A", but the currently higher price of diesel fuel may offset this. An exciting new development in diesel motor homes is the introduction of shorter wheel base, aero-dynamic shaped designs that get better fuel mileage. Time will tell about the popularity of these smaller coaches.

On the down side, diesel engine maintenance is more expensive and complicated than a gasoline engine motor home. Oil changes require about 20 plus quarts of oil plus replacement of a fuel/water separator filter. The recommendation is that this two hundred and fifty dollar service be performed annually. The heavy-duty transmission in the pusher requires fluid and filter changes to the tune of about three hundred dollars every several years. There are driers in the air brake system that will need replacement every few years as well. Most diesels, and now the larger gas coaches, have 22.5 inch wheels with tires in the four to five hundred dollar each range that must be replaced every five to seven years. The cost of this maintenance must be figured into your budget.

Next up is the Gasoline engine motor home. In recent years, these coaches can have up to a twenty-six thousand pound gross vehicle weight chassis. This is the same as many lower end diesel coaches. They can have as many as four slide rooms and boast most of the amenities of a diesel coach. These are front engine designs using mostly Ford or Chevrolet large displacement truck based motors. A big advantage is that they can be serviced at most Ford and Chevrolet dealerships. Periodic oil changes are much less expensive than on a diesel coach. They are typically about forty thousand dollars less expensive than a diesel coach of similar size.

Negatives about gas coaches are poor hill climbing ability compared to the high torque diesel coach. Fuel mileage is also typically several miles per gallon less. Both the last statements are magnified when towing the extra weight of a car. I haven't seen any gas rigs with air suspension or air brakes either.

Class "B" Motor Home

Class B motor homes have been called camper vans or van campers. I guess Kathy and I started RVing back in 1970 when we purchased a used VW Camper bus. We took it to Italy when I was stationed there and it was camped in plenty. We even bought another when we returned. I'm not sure this was the forerunner to the Class B, but it did seem so.

Of the three types of motorized RVs, Class B motor homes are the smallest. Commonly, a minivan or a full size van will be specially customized and turned into a mini RV. There are many professional conversion companies that do an excellent job of converting mini vans and full size vans into RVs. After their conversion, they don't look much different on the outside other than the "bubble top" extension they now have which allows people to walk upright in the interior of the van, and some vans also have a lowered floor to make even more headroom. Most new Class Bs have slide rooms built in them. In the last several years, the Mercedes Benz "Sprinter" cargo van has been introduced in this country. With its diesel power and eighteen to twenty miles per gallon fuel economy, it was a natural to be turned into a class B motor home. There are at least seven or eight companies producing these including Winnebago with a Class B and a beautifully engineered twenty-five foot Class A on a Sprinter chassis. While the Class B may boast most of the amenities of larger coaches, the sheer small size and lack of storage makes them mostly unsuitable for full-time living. Pricing on Class B coaches is rapidly rising above the one hundred thousand dollar mark as well.

Class "C" Motor home

The Class C motor home, or mini motor home, is an RV built on a cut-away van or truck chassis, including the cab. Many Class C motor homes are roughly the size and shape of rental moving trucks. It differs from the Class A motor home in that the Class C chassis comes with the cab from the manufacturer. Another distinguishing feature of the Class C is the bed compartment over the cab. Although that sleeping bunk area in a Class C is typically used for sleeping, not everyone wants to have a bunk bed that they have to climb up in to. In response to this, some manufacturers have made it optional to turn this area into an entertainment system area or storage area. Other manufacturers are building very large Class C motor homes on semi truck chassis. These units are every bit as large, luxurious, and expensive as Class A's. These are known as Super C's.

Class C motor homes come with both gasoline and diesel engines depending on manufacturer and model. The same pro's and con's apply here as in Class A motor homes. The typically lower cost of a Class C makes it quite appealing to full-timers, especially in the thirty-three to thirty-seven foot models. Generally, Class C motor homes cannot carry as much load as a Class A because they are usually built on a van chassis. They also have smaller gas and holding tanks.

Towable RVs

There are numerous choices in Towable RVs available to fit nearly any budget. Because they are towed and don't have their own engine, the prices of some types of most towable RVs are quite reasonable. On the other hand, if you're looking for luxury in a towable, you can find that as well. Deciding which towable RV or camper is right for you will depend on how much towing capacity your current vehicle has. Unless you are going to purchase another vehicle to tow the new RV you are buying, your current vehicle must have the capacity to tow the weight of the unit you desire. This needs to be your number one consideration. You may want a 5th wheel trailer, but unless you have a truck big enough to pull one or have can invest in both the 5th wheel and a new truck, you'll need to consider another type of towable. There are numerous web sites with weight calculators available. Above all else, consult the technical data concerning towing from your vehicle manufacturer. Please do not believe a salesman when he looks at your truck and says, "Sure, your truck can pull this baby". Do your homework!

Fifth Wheel Trailers

The fifth wheel trailer, affectionately known as the "Fiver", is probably the most common towable for full time RVers. The trailer connects to the tow vehicle directly over the bed with a special Fifth Wheel Hitch. This causes several feet of the connected trailer to hang over the tow truck, placing about fifteen to twenty-five percent of the trailer's weight on the rear axle of the truck. Usually the bedroom is located in this raised forward section, but some newer fivers have the living room there. A main advantages of a fifth wheel trailer is that it's easier and safer to tow than travel trailers, but requires more caution and skill than motor homes. They also tend to be easier to back up than travel trailers. Their spacious, open floor plans are quite suitable for full time RVers. Numerous slide-outs provide an almost residential space. They have the most living space of all trailer type RVs, and provide more interior space per foot than a motor home because it does not contain driving and engine compartments. The tow vehicle doubles as local transportation, but large trucks aren't much fun in crowded grocery store parking lots.

On the down side, a fiver doesn't have nearly the storage capacity of a motor home. They may not have the cargo carrying capacity to carry a lot of excess "stuff". Although it is removable, the tow truck requires a fifth wheel hitch in the truck bed. Larger trailers usually require a medium duty truck to provide the power to get them up hills and mountains. The driving and living compartments are separate. The living area is inaccessible while moving. I have seen folks towing cars, boats, and motorcycles and ATV's behind fifth wheel trailers. This is illegal in many states, and provides some interesting handling issues. The larger models can be difficult to maneuver in tight spaces. On tall models, top clearance can be a problem under low branches and structures. It gets worse if there are items on the roof such as canoes.

Travel Trailer
Almost all the pro's and con's associated with fifth wheel trailers apply to the travel trailer except for the method of hitching to the tow vehicle. The travel trailer connects to a hitch ball attached to the frame of the tow vehicle. Heavier units usually require special weight equalizing hitches. Inherently, they are not as stable on the road or as easy to maneuver and park as the fifth wheel trailer.

Toy Hauler
The term toy hauler is applied to both travel trailers and fifth wheel trailers, and it describes an RV designed to carry toys—small cars, dune buggies, four wheelers, motorcycles, etc. A distinguishing

feature of a toy hauler is the large door in the back which opens down to create a ramp, the dedicated garage area or fold-away furniture in the main living compartment, and usually a third axle to support the heavy toys. That space can also be used as a second bedroom with beds dropping from the ceiling on rails. They also make a great office, craft room, and workshop. There are a few motor homes set up as toy haulers also.

Chapter 13 What is The Buying Process?

The buying process can be a relatively good experience if you have done your homework, chosen the right rig for your lifestyle, and are armed with knowledge about the process itself. Some folks we know have likened it to torture. We had quite a different experience. We knew exactly what we wanted in a rig and we knew we wanted a late model diesel pusher. We had researched brands and product lines within brands. After having lived with that first (and only) RV for more than seven years, we are still satisfied with our buying decision.

We were armed with "The RV Buyer's Survival Guide" by Bob Randall and had read it several times. I can't emphasize enough that this small book is an RV buying "Bible" and is available at The RV Bookstore http://rvbookstore.com/ . The sections on figuring MSRP and understanding trade-in values are worth the $14.95 price of the entire book.

By the time you are ready to enter into the buying process, you should have decided on no more than two rigs, preferably one. You should then only discuss the buying price of that RV. If you have a trade, you must save that negotiation for later. Unfortunately, many RV dealerships use the "four-square" method of figuring a price. They will divide a piece of paper into four squares and one will be your trade, one will be the RV you want, one will be the finance details, and the last will have the final price based on all of those details. Don't fall for that. If you are asked "How much can you afford each month", do not answer. Instead, insist on a selling price somewhere between the initial asking price and your initial purchase price based on your homework.

This is a good time to remind you that RV dealerships, like every for-profit business, must make a profit in order to stay in business. They must make money over and above their original purchase price on the unit. My feeling is that five percent is a good figure, considering this will be a major purchase. As the negotiation progresses, you should get to an acceptable purchase price that you are willing to make a buying decision on the spot. After all, you have done a ton of homework to get to this point. Then you will have to deal with your trade-in.

The best possible solution is to sell it yourself. When you trade at a dealership, you add a middleman, the dealer, who will have to profit from the transaction. That's more money out of your pocket. You must realize that you will want more than the dealer will give. Here again, homework is key. There are tools available for evaluating the price of used RVs. Remember that the dealer will want to give you wholesale instead of the higher retail value. This is why you want to avoid mixing the rig price and the trade-in price. So, now you have a purchase price you can live with and there is handshaking all around.

Not so fast. You must demand that this price is only valid upon a satisfactory PDI (Pre-Delivery Inspection). This is a thorough inspection of every aspect of the RV from the roof to the basement, headlights to tail lights. All equipment such as air conditioners, refrigerators and other appliances, slide rooms, driver controls and all water and electric systems must be operated and work as if new. The PDI should be performed on both new and pre-owned units. Some less than scrupulous dealers will try to charge you for this vital service. Don't fall for that, it's a deal breaker. You must demand this be put in writing on the purchase contract. If discrepancies are found during the PDI, the dealer must fix them prior to purchase. Once past this hurdle, you have finished the "front end" of the deal.

Now you are entering the "back end" of the deal. This is where the dealership really makes money. You will be moved to another office to talk with the Finance Manager. Are we having fun yet? The finance manager will explain the various means of financing your RV and introduce several banks and finance companies that he works with. Please remember, we are now introducing another "middle-man" into the transaction that will ultimately be paid by you, the RV buyer.

Part of your homework is to obtain pre-approved financing. Remember that in addition to the price of the RV, there will be taxes and licensing fees. This is also a good time to remember that not all finance companies will loan to full-time RVers without a permanent "sticks and bricks" address. Usually banks won't, but many credit unions will. This is all part of your advance preparation.

The next thing on the Finance Manager's agenda will be the extended warranty. He will have at least one company that will offer several levels of extended warranty coverage on your RV. Because we drive a diesel pusher with lots of on-board electronics and expensive appliances, I recommend an extended warranty. We are on our second one and we have gotten our money's worth. There are, however, some considerations. I would also do some homework to investigate several of the warranty companies and compare both prices and coverage. Visit some RV forums and ask about other folks' experience with different companies. We should have done this, but I didn't. When renewal time came along, we had done the investigation and I believe we picked a good one.

The Finance Manager will now try to sell you a roadside assistance plan and/or towing insurance. We have found through tough and expensive experience that the best company for this is Coach-Net. They are RV pros. They will also know what equipment is required to tow your particular RV. Many folks like the towing and roadside insurance from Good Sam.

Next up for the Finance Manager will usually be insurance. Some larger dealerships have in-house insurance agents. Once again, you should have already picked an insurance company for both vehicle insurance and the extended warranty. This is a good time to remind you that not all insurance companies will write coverage for full-timers.

At long last you have jumped through all the hoops and are ready to take delivery on your new (to you) RV. If you are trading in a rig, there should be a space set aside for that with both rigs side-by-side to facilitate moving all your stuff from one to the other. There should also be an opportunity for a technician to come over to the new rig to explain all the various features and systems as well as point out all the documentation you will receive. Try to spend a night at the dealership so you can then try all this stuff out for yourself. Don't leave the dealership until you are satisfied. Are you tired yet? Buying a rig can be an exhausting experience, but immensely satisfying if you have done your homework and end up with the RV of your dreams.

Chapter 14 What do You Need in Your RV?

This is a listing of the interior stuff Kathy considers essential for enjoying the RV lifestyle.

Stuff to Cook With

This is a very personal decision. I'm not a gourmet cook so I do not have a big mixer, or a food processor and it is no big deal to me. However, you will need pots and pans, plastic glasses and dishware, silverware, serving dishes, storage containers and utensils, and almost everything you would use at home to cook and eat simple meals. Some rigs have much more space in the kitchen area than others, so consider what you will need. If you don't own an RV or you are moving up to a bigger unit, consider this area. We don't eat out a lot, so cooking space is important. The pantry in the RV is small, however you can always find a store to buy groceries, and with a little planning, it's not hard to keep things from overflowing. A good rule of thumb is "a place for everything and everything in its place." When we first started out I had enough food for what seemed to be about three years of eating. I have learned to cut it down, and every six months I will go through the pantry and get rid of things I have not used in the last six months or that have expired. Organizing the pantry is quite simple. Most weeks we eat about the same meals; we have our favorites, so I always check to make sure I have plenty of the ingredients for those. Then there are times I want to make something special, so I take a list to the store and purchase just what I need for that meal. I always have some snacks on hand for when people come by and we are sitting outside talking. Cheese and crackers or cookies work well for that. We also keep a cooler outside the rig for drinks. This gives us more room in the refrigerator. It's really up to you what you have on hand. Some parks will have a box for the local food bank so nothing is lost. Many RVs will have a double door refrigerator, but these are not the same size as the home ones. They can hold about 4-5 bags of cold groceries and we all seem to have way too much anyway.

You will have both a convection oven and a two or three burner stove top and maybe even a propane oven. I have very rarely used the propane oven, other than for storage. I use just the convection oven for any baking I want to do. The only thing I miss is a broiler as the convection oven doesn't have one. I would only use one three to four times a year, so it's no big problem for me.

Stuff to Read

If you enjoy reading consider a Kindle or some other type electronic book reader. There is not much space for lots of books. However, almost every campground has a small library which is usually a "bring one, take one" swap. I have found some great books in these libraries. I take one, read it and pass it on to the next campground, then pick up a new one. It's a great place to get rid of the extra books you may have. They will also have DVD's, CD's and VCR movies, and puzzles to borrow. You will never be bored with nothing to do on a rainy day. We know of one guy who loves to do puzzles, but there was no place to do them in the rig. He couldn't leave it on the table, so he placed a piece of Plexiglas over the puzzle on the table when it was time for dinner. The puzzle is safe and there is peace in the family. That works for him.

Stuff for an Office

Most rigs do not have an office or desk. Finding space to do the computer work can be difficult. We have a side entry on our motor home so the passenger seat area is where our desk is. We bought a collapsible table and store it alongside the sofa when we are traveling, then pull it out and set it up in front of the passenger seat when we are stopped. We actually have two foldable tables. I use one to bead on, and our dining table is used for dinning. There are many places that will build a custom cabinet or desk for you.

Stuff in the Living Area

One of my big pet peeves is that the TVs in most motor homes are up above the driver's seat. I about broke my neck watching TV because the sofa faced the right side of the rig and the TV was to the left. To solve this problem, we had the TV moved from the front and put along the side with a cabinet underneath, then exchanged the sofa for two Lazyboy chairs. It is very comfortable now - feels just like a real living room. The place where the TV was previously is now storage where we keep our travel books. They did a beautiful job, and we are pleased with it. Think outside the box for what you need and be creative. This is your home, so just as you might remodel your stick and brick home, you can remodel your home on wheels.

Stuff to Wear

Life on the road is very simple. Summer is shorts, tee shirts and sandals, winter clothes are jeans, sweatshirts, wind breaker jackets and tennis shoes. We like to attend church, so I have a nice pair of slacks and several tops. Since we don't stay to long in one place, there is no need for an extensive wardrobe. We store the winter clothes under the bed in the summer and the summer clothes there in the winter. It's not too far away if the weather changes. I really dislike Laundromats, so we have a combo washer/dryer in the rig that I use all the time. I really like it, and so far, we have had no problems. But it does take up a lot of space. Many campgrounds will have a coin laundry so you will not have to go into town to do the laundry. Laundromats are not always located in the safest part of town. Most are coin operated, but a new trend is a card much like a credit card. You purchase the card at the camp store, then put money on the card and use this instead of quarters. There are several companies doing this so not every campground will have the same system. I think it would be a great idea if they did. I have the card in a sleeve and write on it which campground it is good for. Just remember to keep saving your quarters.

Stuff to Socialize With

There seems to be an unwritten rule for socializing. If the door to the rig is closed that means company is not welcome. If it is open or you see people moving about, than come knock on the door. With the rigs being so small, it is not often as neat and tidy as your host would like, and you don't want to embarrass your newfound friend. This mostly applies in good weather. Most socializing is done outdoors. Be sure to have 4 chairs so everyone has a seat. Or if you invite someone over, ask them to bring their chairs. We have a gadget called Campfire in a Can that is a small container that is a propane burner with artificial logs. It is just like having a small campfire; when you are done, just turn off the propane and the fire goes out. We have roasted marshmallows and cooked hot dogs on it. It works for us. Transporting wood from one state to another is now prohibited in the west as there is a western pine beetle that is eating up the pine trees. They are trying to contain it by not allowing firewood of any kind to be brought in from different states. Please be aware of what can happen if you bring wood from somewhere else. There is firewood for sale everywhere open fires are allowed. Help to be an asset to our wonderful forests.

We have found that our ideas about a lot of the stuff we thought we would need just weren't true. This lifestyle is quite simple and your camping friends are just happy to hang out with you. The type and style of clothing is not important. Being comfortable is what is important, and having a tee shirt from all the places you have been is a great conversation starter. I have a shirt from Bryce Canyon that has started many conversations. People either have been there or want to go or they will tell you of a similar park they have been to and enjoyed. Of course you have to add that to your bucket list.

Chapter 15 What Other Stuff Will You Need?

This chapter contains all the things that John feels are essential for a well-equipped RV.

Tow Gear for Towed Vehicle

Before towing any vehicle, make certain that it can be towed with all four wheels on the ground, without damage to the transmission. There are Dinghy Towing Guides published annually by Motor Home Magazine and Family Motor Coaching Association that give information on what cars may be towed four down. Before you make a decision, refer to the owner's manual for the particular vehicle and year of manufacture.

Tow Bar or Tow Dolly

Most of the rigs I see towing are using a tow bar and towing the car four wheels down. It's quick and easy to connect (with some practice), it usually stores on the motor home, and it's relatively lightweight. On the other hand a tow dolly is good for those folks who want to tow multiple vehicles without having to install a mounting bracket on each one. It also is the best way to tow a vehicle that can't be towed four down without modification. Modifications can include a transmission lube pump system or a driveline disconnect device. If you decide to tow a vehicle whose manufacturer says that it is not towable four down, the vehicle warranty will surely be voided if you have a problem caused by towing. The aftermarket transmission lubrication pump circulates transmission fluid throughout the transmission and keeps the gears lubed. For rear wheel drive cars, the driveshaft disconnect keeps the transmission from rotating. These modifications are not cheap, running about eight hundred to a thousand dollars including labor. The downside for a tow dolly or trailer is the initial expense and where to put it when you are camped.

There are two basic tow bar designs. The most common is mounted to the hitch receiver on the motor home; the other is permanently mounted to the dinghy vehicle. The former has collapsible arms which slide back and forth, making them easy to connect. As you drive away, the arms automatically extend, self-center and lock in place. The car mounted tow bar hooks up to the motor home with a ball type hitch mounted on the motor home.

When it is not in use, it can be removed completely or folded against the vehicle for quick, compact storage.

Just as the hitch receiver has a weight rating for the maximum weight that can be towed by the motor home, the tow bar is rated at a specific weight capacity. Whichever tow bar you choose, be sure it is rated above the weight of your towed vehicle, plus its contents. Look for a ten to fifteen percent cushion on top of the dinghy and its load.

Mounting Bracket

No matter what kind of tow bar you choose, you must have a mounting bracket attached to the car. The mounting bracket's purpose is to connect the tow bar to the towed vehicle. Each bracket is custom-designed to fit a specific vehicle or range of vehicles, and is attached to the frame, sub frame, core support or other points along the vehicle's undercarriage with bolts torqued to a specific value. These bolts should be checked periodically to make sure they are tight.

The two types of mounting brackets are exposed and hidden. The visible portions of exposed brackets are fixed while the attachment points on hidden brackets are easily removed when the vehicle is not being towed. Hidden brackets are preferred because they are do not show or stick out and impale your knee or shin when the vehicle is not being towed.

Auxiliary Brake Controller

Motor home brakes aren't built to stop the additional weight of a towed vehicle. They're made to stop the coach and its contents. But even if you had extra braking capacity, the weight of the towed vehicle is not riding on the motor home chassis. It's pushing on it from behind.

Supplemental or auxiliary brakes also relieve stress on the tow bar and the mounting brackets. They also keep the rig and the towed vehicle straight as you brake, so there's less chance of a "jackknife." Supplemental brakes also reduce the chance of a motor home service brake failure as a result of sustained braking such as when you're driving down a steep grade in the mountains.

According to literature from Roadmaster, Inc., some motor home chassis manufacturers will void your warranty, and insurance adjusters will void your policy against damage claims if you tow without supplemental brakes. Workhorse will void your chassis warranty if you tow more than 1,000 pounds without supplemental brakes; Ford stipulates 1,500 pounds.

Most states require some form of supplemental braking when towing, although the minimum vehicle weight will vary from state to state. That information is available on the Roadmaster, Inc. website http://roadmasterinc.com/ .

Some auxiliary braking systems are a box with an actuator that is connected to the dinghy's brake pedal. The box sits on the floor in front of the driver's seat. It will require power supplied through a twelve volt receptacle. Often there will be a remote communications device to let you know the condition of the system from the driver's seat of the coach. There should also be an emergency break-away switch on the dinghy connected to the coach. In case of a failure of the tow bar, the break-away switch will be activated and apply the dinghy brakes.

Other systems mount under the hood of the dinghy and use either air from the coach air brake system or react to hydraulic pressure in a gas coach brake system. There are many other systems available. We use the box system as it can be quickly moved from car to car when we change.

There are also auxiliary brake controllers for use with trailer brakes. An electric trailer brake controller supplies power from the tow vehicle to the trailer's electric brakes. Many styles are available that differ from how they look, to the number of brakes they can power, but all of them can be divided up into two main groups, proportional or time delayed.

A proportional brake controller senses how quickly the tow vehicle is stopping and applies the same amount of braking power to the trailer. With a time delayed or solid state brake controller, stepping on the vehicle brakes causes a predetermined amount of braking power to be sent to the trailer and then there is a delay as the unit ramps up to full braking power.

Hitch Equipment for Your Towing Vehicle
If you will tow a trailer, you will need to equip your tow vehicle with the proper equipment for the type and weight of your trailer.

Travel Trailer

A weight distribution hitch system takes the center of the weight off of your trailer hitch and distributes it between the tow vehicle and the trailer wheels. Rather than merely supporting the trailer tongue weight, weight distributing hitches apply leverage between the towing vehicle and trailer causing the tongue weight to be carried by all axles of both the tow vehicle and the trailer.

Fifth Wheel Trailer

A fifth wheel hitch offers a number of advantages over other types of hitches. Some of these are: towing capacity, safety, maneuverability and stability. Fifth wheel hitches are a special class of hitch that mounts over or forward of the rear axle of the towing vehicle. The vehicle being towed has a king pin on the end of the trailer which fits into the specially designed notch on the fifth wheel hitch. Since the fifth wheel hitch rests in the bed of the pickup truck, this sometimes presents a challenge because the bed is not very useful for hauling or storing anything else. The length of the bed also comes into play because when backing up, it is possible to jackknife and join trailer to truck with unacceptable results. For this reason, there is a sliding hitch available for short-bed pickup trucks to avoid this. Another issue is that the normal tailgate of the pickup must be removed to use a fifth wheel hitch. There are, of course, accessories that are specially designed to work with these types of trailers and solve many issues.

Water Filters, Hoses and Sewer Equipment

Most RVers will quickly accumulate an assortment of sewer and water hoses along with some sort of fresh water filter.

Water Filtration and Treatment

Most late model motor homes and fifth wheel trailers have "whole house" water filters plumbed in, usually located near the water/sewer service bay. The filter element of choice in these is a sediment filter. Water with noticeable haze or murkiness is carrying particulate matter that is referred to as sediment. Large particles settle out of water pretty fast, so what water is carrying are very small particles. Besides the noticeable effect on water clarity, sediment can also create problems by plugging up other filters you may be using, causing them to fail prematurely.

Sediment or "sed filters" are measured in "microns" or one thousandth of a millimeter. A twenty micron filter will remove particles twenty microns or larger in diameter, while a five micron filter will remove sediment five microns or bigger. Sediment filters strain out the sediment and hold it. At some point, the filter is plugged and must either be cleaned (if possible) or replaced.

A sediment filter should always be the first filter in a filter system. It will protect your other downstream equipment from premature failure by removing the junk that could cause a problem.

The things that affect taste and odor of water will go right through a sediment filter, so you must use something else to remove them. Enter the carbon filter. The carbon can grab onto the bad stuff in water, leaving it clean-tasting and odor-free. It can only pull out a fixed amount of contaminants, so it will not last forever. You can't clean a carbon filter, so you must replace it when full or when water pressure and flow drop to an unacceptable level. Usually, carbon filters will last twice as long as sediment filters, but they're also more expensive.

In my own water filter system, I use a ten micron sediment filter followed by a one micron sediment filter and follow that up with a carbon filter. The filter canisters are standard household units bought from a hardware store and plumbed together with brass fittings. This filter follows a water pressure regulator to maintain no more than fifty pounds per square inch of water pressure. Some parks have much higher pressure that can damage RV plumbing if not regulated. The regulated and filtered water is connected to the coach water inlet port. I have placed a "Y" valve just prior to the entrance to the filter so unfiltered water goes to the black tank flush inlet. Someplace in that water line to the black tank flush should be a backflow preventer device, also available at a hardware store. That will prevent the possibility of black water coming back down the line and contaminating your fresh water and filter system.

Rigs with automatic icemakers installed often have a filter in-line to the ice-maker. There may also be a separate spigot on the sink to dispense filtered water. That filter, available at Camping World, must be replaced periodically. We change ours every three months.

The whole house filter(s) must also be changed as they get filled with sediment and other contaminants. Check the first sediment filter every several weeks and look for a brown color throughout the filter media. That is the time to change it out. If it is very bad, check the next filter in line also. Carbon filters only last three months in our system.

If you find yourself in an area with high sodium (salt) content in the water, none of the above filters will remove the salt from the water.

Enter the reverse osmosis (RO) water filter system. It uses a semi-permeable plastic membrane to filter out most of the contaminants in water, including almost all biologic pathogens, minerals and salts, and some other chemical contaminants. The output side of the membrane produces pure water. The waste, dissolved solids, and contaminants which are called brine, are flushed down a drain. The costs for an RO system are much higher than regular filtration, but may be the only answer unless you buy bottled water.

We carried a water softener for the first four years on the road. It was a black plastic thing that looked like a miniature fire hydrant. It came with hardness test strips, so I know it worked to reduce the calcium content in hard water. This calcium build-up can be a real problem for RV water heaters. The calcium crystals form and flow through the fresh water system and clog the aerators in sink faucets. They are easy to clean, but it's inconvenient to have to do this every other day or so. The same goes for RV washing machines. Unfortunately, our softener was heavy (sixty five pounds) and only treated three hundred gallons before needing to be recharged with rock salt pellets. That container was another forty pounds or so and took up a lot of space. Consequently, we sold it. Newer units use table salt and treat up to two thousand gallons. We're looking into these.

Fresh Water Hoses, Pressure Regulators, Etc.

Plastic or rubber garden hoses are not suitable for fresh water use. The hoses you use for supplying fresh water to your rig should be purpose designed for supplying fresh potable water. They are constructed so they won't impart taste or odor to the water.

Typically these hoses come in either one half inch or five eighths inch diameter and in various lengths up to one hundred feet. The larger diameter hose will provide more flow and are the best choice. We carry two twenty-five foot hoses. Most campsites will only require one length, but some need more. I would not want to have most of a fifty foot hose coiled up under my rig. Other shorter lengths of four to ten feet are useful for hooking up filters and for bypassing them if necessary. If you use a hose to flush your holding tanks, use one made in other colors than your fresh water hoses. The same goes for hoses used to wash your rig. We use a fifty foot green plastic garden hose for that purpose. When you buy fittings such as "Y" connectors and shut-off valves, avoid the temptation to go cheap and use plastic ones. Spend a little more and buy brass fittings, and you won't be surprised some night when one of them lets go and you have a high pressure flood on your hands. This is the voice of experience talking.

There are special drinking water hoses made especially for cold weather use. They have a heating element permanently woven into the hose and use electricity from the power pedestal to keep the hose from freezing if the outside temperature drops below freezing during the night. They are expensive costing as much as one hundred dollars for a twenty-five foot length. We try to avoid areas where this might happen, but we aren't always successful. A less expensive and quite effective method is to purchase an electrical "heat tape" and connect it to the length of the hose. These usually have a thermostat that activates when the temperature drops past a set limit. Cover that up with inexpensive pipe insulation and you won't have problems with your hose freezing.

When you pack up to depart your campsite, blow all the water out of your hoses and roll them up with the ends screwed together. This will keep them sanitary and easy to store. If at all possible, do not store fresh water hoses in the same compartment as sewer hoses and fittings. This could possibly result in some nasty consequences. Poop and drinking water should never mix. Enough said about that.

A water pressure regulator reduces the park water pressure down to less than fifty pounds per square inch, forty being preferable. This is to prevent high water pressure from damaging plumbing lines and fittings buried deep down in the bowels of your rig, and keep it from flooding. A good water pressure regulator will reduce pressure but allow maximum flow, thus ensuring an adequate shower pressure. Most will have a gauge to measure the outlet pressure and can be adjusted to your desired pressure. This type of regulator should cost somewhere in the fifty to sixty-five dollar range.

Sewer Hoses, Etc.

No matter what the rig, you must dump that pesky black tank from time to time. Sewer hoses come in a rainbow of colors and many lengths and thicknesses. Some press fit together, and some use bayonet type fittings. I prefer the positive locking bayonet type coupling as it will not pull apart. The material used for the hose should be as thick as you can find. Hose sidewall material ranges from 10 mils thick to over forty. The thicker material is much better. The thin stuff can develop pinhole leaks that can spoil your day. Usually, the sidewall material is stretched over a coiled metal wire so the hose can be compressed for storage. Unfortunately, when stepped on, these hoses will never be round again. A new material has no metal coil and can be compressed and stepped on and will return to the original shape. These hoses come in ten to fifteen foot lengths. We carry three ten footers and one fifteen footer. There have been several occasions where we have had to use all of it to reach the sewer connection.

An essential accessory is a threaded connection to the sewer with a bayonet fitting on the other end for the hose. Some municipalities require a rubber "doughnut" fitting between hose and sewer hole, so keep one on hand. Other places require the sewer hose to be supported several inches above the ground. We have a "slinky" device for this as well as a length of plastic gutter and PVC supports for longer runs. You should also have caps for both ends of each hose to keep things clean and dry in the compartment where your sewer gear is stored.

This seems like a good time to remind you that the black water holding tank in your rig has a three inch opening to the sewer valve. Thirty or forty gallons of black water sludge can gravity feed through that opening at an alarming rate. This is why you want to double check all your sewer connections before you open that valve. It's amazing how much of that tank will empty on the ground before you can reach the valve to close it. "I'm just saying".

Another method of dumping the black holding tank is the electric macerator. This is a twelve volt device very much like a sink disposer. A motor turns a set of metal knives to chop and shred all solids coming down the line and then pump it out a garden hose sized hose to the dump. It can also pump uphill several feet as well as quite a long distance. A great advantage to an electric macerator is if you are parked next to a house. You can run the hose to a sewer clean-out and evacuate your tanks. These range in price from two to four hundred dollars.

Electrical Surge Protection

In our opinion, all RVs should be protected from power surges as well as over and under voltages. A power surge or a lightning strike on power lines can destroy electrical and electronic items in your coach such as stereos, satellites, microwaves, televisions and refrigerators. Surge protection is protection against voltage spikes on power lines. Direct lightning strikes are so catastrophic that no device can effectively protect against a close or direct lightning strike. Over or under voltage protection is effective for a gradual increase or decrease in voltage, exceeding the maximum or minimum voltage for which appliances are rated. Over voltage and under voltage protection removes primary power from the RV when the voltage drops below 102V or above 132V (safe mode).

There is a wealth of safety information by Mike Sokol available at The No-Shock Zone http://www.noshockzone.org/15/ He discusses how bad wiring at RV parks kills people every year.

Devices are available that can protect from these conditions as well as improperly wired electrical pedestals in RV parks. They can be directly wired into the RV or connected to the electrical pedestal and the RV plugged into the protective device. If you have a fifty amp electrical system in your rig, be sure to purchase a fifty amp power protector. A good place to look for these is at Camping World or the RV Upgrade Store www.rvupgradestore.com .

Ultra Violet Radiation Protective Covers

Ultra Violet Radiation, or UV, will damage surfaces exposed to constant sunlight.

Windows

The windshield of a motor home will expose all seats and dashboard areas to this. UV resistant covers can be made to fit any motor home and are sold in sets that include the front side windows as well as the windshield. A side benefit is that they will keep the rig cooler. Large windows on fifth wheel trailers can also benefit from these covers. They can be made to fit inside the rig with suction cups, or outside with snap or twist fittings. There are also covers available for side mirrors and windshield wipers.

Tires

Tires are especially susceptible to premature aging due to UV radiation. White tire covers will protect them as well as keep them cooler than black covers. Some attach over each tire with stretch cords to keep them on. Others attach to the outside of the rig with snaps or other fasteners. I think the latter are far easier to attach and take off.

Outdoor Gear

This is the stuff you need to enjoy your campsite when the weather is good.

Seating

The first thing that comes to mind is outdoor seating, either as chairs or lounges. Just remember that the large lounges can be hard to store. We prefer the director style chairs as we find them to be more comfortable than the "bag" style chairs. They cost a little more, but some even have built-in trays for drinks and snacks. Whatever you buy, remember that you must find room for it somewhere in the rig or towed vehicle. We recommend sitting in a lot of different chairs to get the most comfortable "sit".

Tables

We have several folding tables to use when we go to flea markets and sell our bead products. We have two four footers and a small two by two foot table we used to use for our radio show. Now, we use one of the four foot tables for the grill. Our experience with campground picnic tables has been mixed. Some are nice, six or more feet long and made of artificial materials. Most however are old wooden tables with plenty of splinters. We have a heavy duty vinyl cover for six foot picnic tables and matching covers for the seats. We use it often. This is dependent on there being tables at all. Our experience is about half of the campgrounds we visit have them.

Grills

We believe a good outdoor grill is an essential piece of gear for the full time RVer. A key consideration is finding storage space for the grill. If you have plenty of room in your pickup truck for a large home style grill, bring it along. Most of us will have to live with smaller portable grills that will fit in basement storage compartments. We keep ours in a large plastic tub to keep grease and other debris away from the storage compartment. These grills can cost as little as ten dollars for a cheap charcoal model to over five hundred for a deluxe stainless steel beauty. By far, most of the grills we see in campgrounds are propane gas models. We used a WalMart low end model that cost around thirty dollars. I was on number four after almost eight years on the road when the bottom rusted out. We now are the proud owners of a Webber Q model 120. We also use a twenty pound gas bottle instead of the one pound canisters because we can refill the bottle much more economically than constantly purchasing the canisters. From what I have found in campgrounds and in internet surveys, the Coleman "Road Trip" and the Webber "Baby Q" like ours are the most popular gas grills in use by full timers.

Portable Campfire

I included this item because we have one, and I am starting to see more and more of them appear in campgrounds. The brand name is "Little Red Campfire" or Campfire in a Can". It is basically a propane gas burner with ceramic fire logs on top. You remove the red top and unwind the gas hose and regulator. Hook it up to a propane source and light it and you have an instant campfire. We always ask if we can use it in areas where there are "No Open Fires Allowed" signs due to drought conditions. We have not been refused, yet. These little guys put out enough heat to keep your feet warm on cold nights and they draw people in to talk around the campfire.

Propane "Extend-a-Stay"

The Extend-a-Stay can be used for two purposes. First, if you run out of LP gas in your motor home propane tank; and second, to hook up the Extend-a-Stay to an outside LP/propane cylinder. This lets propane gas into your system from the outside cylinder allowing you to have continuous gas supply without having to move your RV and refill your permanent propane tank until you are ready to move. Additionally, you can use LP gas from your propane system to fuel high pressure appliances like grills and camp stoves straight from your RV's permanent LP gas system.

The standard kit includes brass tee fitting and 5' flexible pigtail for hooking up an outside propane cylinder to fuel your RV LP system. The deluxe kit also includes 12' of high pressure appliance hose to fuel your high pressure appliances directly from your RVs LP Gas system.

These kits are available at most RV stores. The standard kit costs around seventy dollars, the deluxe kit is around one hundred dollars. Installation is pretty straightforward if you are handy with tools. Any modification to your LP gas system should include a leak test and a pressure drop test. These tests are best done by a professional.

Ladder

A good ladder is essential for putting up sunscreens as well as washing your rig. The main concern should be the posted weight capacity of the ladder. Flimsy folding ladders contribute to dangerous falls. An RV ladder should be compact enough when folded to store easily. We store our ladder on a rack hanging from the built-in ladder at the rear of the coach. We bought a Werner brand ladder at a hardware store rated for three hundred and fifty pounds.

Safety Equipment

Every RVer needs to take a good look at safety equipment that could possibly save your life.

Flares and Towing Insurance

I'm sure you've seen semi-trucks along the side of the road with three triangular reflectors spaced out behind it. They are there to alert people to move over a lane as the rig is disabled for some reason. These triangles are inexpensive and should be in your RV emergency kit along with several flashlights and road flares to signal a night break down. Obviously, the best piece of emergency equipment is a cell phone to call for help. Hand in hand with the cell phone is towing insurance. We believe the best contracts are available from the Good Sam Club www.goodsamclub.com as well as Coach-Net http://nmc.com/ . Once you are registered with a towing service, they will send a tow truck with the proper equipment to tow your particular rig. They can also provide emergency fuel or change a tire if you have the proper size spare. Most towable RVs either come with a spare tire, or have a place to store one. Some Class B and C motor homes may have spare tires also. Class A motor home tires are large and quite heavy when mounted on a wheel. My motor home has a storage bay that is shaped to hold a spare tire, but the space is better used for tools in my case. If you routinely travel far from regular services, a spare tire may be a good idea. Some RV travel sources recommend you carry an unmounted spare when traveling to Alaska. There are services there to mount a tire, but it isn't likely that your specific size will be available.

Fire Extinguishers

Most RV's come with at least one fire extinguisher, usually of the powder type. This type of extinguisher has a pressure gauge with a red/green indicator. While the gauge may read green, the unit might not function correctly after sitting in one position for a long time; the powder settles and clumps in the bottom of the extinguisher. Pick this type unit up and turn it upside down several times every six months or so to loosen the powder. This is also a good time to check that the gauge is in the green area.

Kathy and I have been to a number of RV safety seminars, including some with live fires to put out. We can't emphasize enough the importance of this vital safety training. It is available at most large rallies. Check out http://macthefireguy.com/ for information on the location and times for this training. We were given advice to have a number of extinguishers on hand. You should have one for your car or truck, one for an outside compartment, one in the bedroom, and one near the kitchen area. These small extinguishers will not put out an RV fire that has been going for more than a couple of minutes. You have them to beat down the flames so you can get out of your rig. Even the largest RV can be reduced to a pile of smoldering ashes in five or six minutes. There are many videos on the internet showing this. For that reason, you must get out quickly. Your "stuff" isn't worth your life or your family's life. These four extra fire extinguishers can be purchased for as little as sixty or seventy dollars.

There are automatic temperature activated units for the both engine and the generator compartments. These use a gas such as Halon to displace the oxygen and extinguish the fire. There is also a Halon unit available for the refrigerator compartment to combat refrigerator fires. These units are expensive, but they provide peace of mind.

Fire Alarms

If your rig has a fire alarm, or smoke detector, test it for proper operation and change the battery at least annually. If not, go out and get one immediately. We have found that the alarm is usually placed outside the bedroom and near the gas range. Consequently, it will go off every time you fry bacon. We switched ours to a unit made by Kidde that has a push button switch that turns the alarm off for ten minutes, and then automatically returns the unit to normal operation. We highly recommend it.

Gas Alarms

Today's RVs have several propane gas appliances including the hot water heater, range top and stove, refrigerator, and at least one gas furnace. Most RVs will have a propane gas alarm mounted near the floor by the kitchen. This is because propane is heavier than air and will sink to the floor. These alarms may be battery operated or permanently connected to twelve volts from the RV battery. In either case, test these units according to the manufacturer's instruction book.

If your rig does not have a carbon monoxide alarm, get one immediately and place it in the sleeping area near head height. Carbon monoxide or CO is odorless and colorless and will displace oxygen. Carbon monoxide gas is produced by combustion such as from a generator set or even an engine running outside your rig. CO can kill you and your loved ones. Don't take a chance without having a functioning CO alarm. Check and replace the alarm battery annually with the smoke detector battery.

Weather Radio

We consider our weather radio an essential piece of emergence equipment. We turn it on and tune to the one of seven frequencies that is strongest, and we get National Weather Service (NOAA) forecasts and severe weather alerts for our area. Our radio also can use the Specific Area Message Encoding (SAME) system. A programmed NWR SAME receiver will turn on for the alert message, with the listener hearing the 1050 Hz warning alarm tone as an attention signal, followed by the broadcast message. At the end of the broadcast message, listeners will hear a brief digital end-of-message static burst followed by a resumption of the National Weather Service broadcast cycle. To program NWR SAME receivers with the proper county(s) and marine area(s) of choice, you need to know the 6-digit SAME code number(s) for that county(s). Once you have the number, follow the directions supplied the manufacturer of your NWR SAME receiver for programming. The number is available either online at the http://www.nws.noaa.gov/nwr/indexnw.htm , or by telephone at 1-888-NWR-SAME (1-888-697-7263) for a voice menu. Your campground management will have information on the name of the surrounding counties. We use a Midland Model WR 120, which has the SAME technology. It retails for about fifty dollars but can be found at many stores for around thirty. We don't always program our radio as it will give broad area information including severe weather alerts constantly. Our radio is on constantly, so we check its internal battery often.

We also use weather apps on our Android smart phone. These are "The Weather Channel" and my favorite, "Radar Now" which uses the built-in GPS and shows live weather radar in your area.

Tools

The selection of tools you carry should be determined by your expertise in fixing RV related systems. This can include tools for working with PVC piping to fix RV plumbing issues; electrical testing devices such as digital voltmeters for troubleshooting electrical problems, an assortment of general purpose tools such as screwdrivers, wrenches, and sockets for general repairs. There are many books available to help with repair of RV systems as well as the manuals that came with the RV for those items. One tool I find invaluable is a two pound short handle sledge hammer for pounding stakes in the ground to anchor awnings and ground mats. Another must-have is a battery powered drill and extra battery. My favorite source for tools and even specialty tools is Harbor Freight Tools http://www.harborfreight.com/ because they have stores across the country as well as internet ordering.

Maps and Navigational Aids

You will not be on the road long before you have a collection of stuff to help you find your way.

Paper Maps

In spite of all the electronic gadgets we have to help us find our way around our beautiful country, paper maps are still handy and can be easily marked up to find your way around. We use a large type road atlas by the American Map Company that we have replaced three times because the pages get dog-eared and torn. We also obtain state maps from the various welcome centers we visit. If you will stay in one state and tour it for an extended time, it is a good idea to buy a detailed state road atlas. We also carry a Motor Carriers Road Atlas available at truck stops. This will have low clearance bridges and hazardous cargo (propane) restrictions listed by state. Last but certainly not least, we have the Mountain Directory East and Mountain Directory West. They list most of the mountain grades of five percent or more that a large truck or motor home might encounter and describes them. This is a lot of weight to carry and store, but it is peace of mind for us as we travel through new territory.

While not exactly a map, we carry a wonderful book called The Next Exit. This is also available as an application for Android and iPhones. The book is divided by state and then by Interstate highways. There is an entry for each exit with information on facilities available and even nearby campgrounds. What makes this guide a "must have" for RVers is that facilities that can accommodate large rigs are printed in red. This way you can look ahead to see where RV friendly stops are located.

Campground Guides

We carry both the Eastern and Western editions of the Woodall's Campground Directories. This gives us information on campgrounds, fairgrounds, state and national parks and other places to camp across the country. Often we refer to it several hours before we stop for the night and call one campground we have found for a reservation. The directory includes prior year's pricing information, number of sites, a description of amenities, phone number and website, and directions to the campground. There is also a campground rating system included to give you ratings on the facilities as well as recreation opportunities near the property. There are other campground guides, but this is the most comprehensive of all. Trailer Life has a similar product, but it will probably be merged with the Woodall's as they are owned by the same company. These are fairly large paper bound books and the information is available on-line at http://www.woodalls.com/ and on a CD. We prefer the paper version as our laptop screen has lots of glare while we are on the road.

We belong to several campground clubs and each one has its own guidebook. We carry a guide for Passport America, RPI, Thousand Trails, Escapees, and several others. Those are mostly used for trip planning.

Electronic Mapping Programs

There are a number of programs that run on a personal computer that are helpful for trip planning as well as providing Global Positioning System (GPS) information in real time. We use Street Atlas from the DeLorme Company, http://www.delorme.com/, mostly for trip planning. Another popular program is Streets and Trips from Microsoft, http://www.microsoft.com/Streets/. Co Pilot Live, http://www.copilotlive.com/, from ALK Technologies is another system that also will run on a PC as well as Android and Apple cell phones and tablets. All these programs require a learning curve to use all the features available, but I find the one I use invaluable to give me information on mileage to travel as well as fuel usage. There are after-market overlay files for use with these programs that will overlay symbols indicating special points of interest such as campground clubs, fuel stops, restaurant chains, and many others of use to RVers. These files are available on the Discovery Owner's Association website, http://www.discoveryowners.com/cginfo.htm and are available free of charge.

Global Positioning System (GPS)

GPS systems for vehicles have been around for years and are quite helpful for directing you in unfamiliar territory. Recently, new models have been introduced specifically for the RVer. They provide input of the height, width, length, and weight of your rig so as to not route you on roads with low bridges and weight restrictions. They also come pre-loaded with many points of interest such as campgrounds and parks as well as fuel sources.

These units are being introduced constantly, and the best bet is to look them up in RV specific publications.

Cellular telephones and tablet computers are often GPS equipped, and there are many applications or apps available for the RVer. I believe the best is an app called "All Stays." This app is available for Android and Apple phones and tablets. We have it running on an Apple iPad and it will indicate campgrounds along the way. When you click on the symbol, all information about that campground will appear as well as reviews by previous campers.

Chapter 16 Where Will We Camp?

OK, you have your RV and you've filled it with all the stuff you need. You're ready to go camping. The question is where to go? My suggestion is to find a place fairly close to home and do a shakedown trip to make sure all the RV systems are working and you have all the "stuff" you will need for a longer trip. Look in your local yellow pages for a campground. It doesn't have to be fancy; it just has to have hook-ups. Hopefully, this first trip will whet your appetite for more and longer RV trips. We're not including boondock camping in this chapter because we have an entire chapter on boon docking.

Public Campgrounds and Resorts

These are largely privately owned properties designated as public access campgrounds. Most of these are not affiliated with larger camping companies such as Kampgrounds of America (KOA) or Yogi Bear's Jellystone Park. We have found that the best resource for finding campgrounds is the Woodall's Campground Directory. There are so many campgrounds that the book is now split into an Eastern and a Western edition. When we are travelling between destinations, we use the Woodall's constantly to find a campground close to the highway and with whatever amenities we need. The book will also have ratings and year old prices. Lately we have been using an iPad application called All Stays that works with the embedded GPS to show campgrounds as a symbol along our route. When we click on the symbol, a dialog box opens with information about that campground as well as reviews from prior campers. This app helps us to make more informed decisions before we stop for a night or even a week.

When we're travelling from point to point, we usually don't need much in the way of hook-ups other than electric and maybe water. We also prefer a pull-through site so we can get in and out quickly. We usually make a decision about stopping around two o'clock and call the selected campground for a reservation.

Sometimes we decide to stay for several days or a week at a "destination" campground. This is a campground close to a large city, a national park or other attraction; or a park so full of amenities and special features that it is a destination unto itself. A good example of a destination park is Cherry Hill Park in College Park, MD. Cherry Hill is the closest RV Park to Washington, DC

and all of its attractions. Check it out at
http://www.cherryhillpark.com/ .

Next are the affiliate groups of campgrounds such as KOA
http://koa.com/ , Yogi Bear http://www.campjellystone.com/ ,
Best Parks in America http://www.bestparksinamerica.com/ and
others. These campgrounds usually have similar amenities and
rules, and also will have a map or book listing all the parks in that
system. The three systems above are located all across the country.
We have found most of these parks to be quite nice, but more
expensive than independently owned campgrounds.

You owe it to yourself to check out all these types of campgrounds
and decide what works for you.

Membership Camping Clubs

I guess you could call membership camping clubs as the "Vacation
Condo timeshares" of the RV world. You pay an upfront fee, or
initiation fee, or whatever the particular group calls it. In any case,
most of these will be in the thousands of dollars. Then there will
be a yearly "maintenance fee" or dues. This will probably be in the
hundreds of dollars. For that money, you can camp at the
properties included in their catalog. Generally there will be
conditions such as the requirement to be out of the system for a
certain number of days. There may be small daily fees for utilities.
All of them require signing a contract that obligates you to pay
whether you use the facilities or not. The recent economic
downturn has not been kind to some of these operations. Most are
cash strapped and campground maintenance is deferred in some
cases. Our recommendation is to wait at least a year before
committing to any of these. That will give you time to talk with
folks who have these contracts and decide if they are for you.

The only exception is Passport America (PA)
http://passportamerica.com/ . We suggest you join this club as
soon as possible. The dues are currently $44 per year. PA has
signed up almost eighteen hundred RV parks across the country to
give you fifty per cent off nightly rates on camping. There may be
conditions such as no discounts during "high season" or discounts
only good for one or two nights. No matter what, you will get your
money back after only two or three nights of camping. We have
used PA parks all over the country and we have been quite happy

with the membership. PA will send you their large catalog of participating parks. There will be descriptions of the park and directions. There will also be notes about the PA rate and any exceptions.

Good Sam and Coast to Coast
Good Sam, or the Good Sam Club http://www.goodsamclub.com/ , is owned by the Affinity Group, also parent company to Camping World, Coast to Coast, and Motor Home and Trailer Life magazines. The Good Sam Club has signed up several thousand campgrounds that will give five to ten per cent discounts to members. Club membership also includes membership in the Camping World President's Club with ten per cent discounts at Camping World stores.

Coast to Coast http://www.coastresorts.com/ is a membership club providing camping for ten dollars a night at over two hundred private resort style campgrounds. You also can camp for fifteen dollars a night at nearly two hundred more Coast Good Neighbor Parks. To become a Coast to Coast member, you first must join any one of the affiliated private membership campgrounds which becomes your "home resort." Once you join the home resort, you are then eligible to become a Coast to Coast member.

RPI
RPI or Resort Parks International http://resortparks.com/ provides access to their network of private affiliated RPI and RPI Preferred RV resorts. The membership is only available to individuals whose home resort is affiliated with RPI. You pay ten dollars per night for an RV site. You may stay at each resort up to seven days twice a year and return to the same resort in as little as seven days between visits. You may stay at any of the affiliated resorts located outside a 125-air mile radius from your home.

Thousand Trails
Thousand Trails (TT) http://www.thousandtrails.com/ is now owned and operated by Equity Lifestyles Properties, known as ELS. ELS is the owner of several hundred resorts under the Encore http://www.rvonthego.com/ brand. Gradually these will all be under one roof. At present there are about eighty TT parks around the country. TT has developed a Zone Pass where you can use the parks in one of four geographic zones for $499 every year.

This gets you thirty nights at no additional charge. Nights over thirty will be $3 per night. This seems like a good program if you are camping in only one area of the country. Other memberships that include all parks in the system are also available at considerably higher cost but with no nightly fees.

Western Horizons

Western Horizons Resorts http://westernhorizonresorts.com/ operates 18 resorts and two affiliated camping networks: Sunbelt USA http://sunbeltrvcamping.com/ and Adventure Outdoor Resorts http://www.aorcamping.com/ . Western Horizons requires a onetime fee and annual dues.

Escapees RV Club

The Escapees RV Club http://www.escapees.com/ has nineteen campgrounds. About half are owned by the club and the rest are cooperative ventures built and financed by Escapees members. Nightly fees average $15 per night. You must be a member of the Escapees RV Club to use these parks, and membership is currently about $80 per year which includes a wonderful magazine. This is the premier RV club for full and long time RV'ers. They also operate a world class mail forwarding service from headquarters in Livingston, TX. We love Escapees and are lifetime members. If you decide to join, please reference our member number 88896 on the application.

National Parks

Many of our wonderful National Parks have campgrounds. A lot of the National Park campgrounds were built by the Civilian Conservation Corps in the nineteen thirties. Many are primitive, but some have been upgraded and have full hook-ups and can accommodate large RV's. Go to http://www.nps.gov/ for information on all of the National Parks and what facilities are available.

National Forests and Grasslands

Go to http://www.fs.fed.us/ to find camping opportunities in our National Forests and National Grasslands.

State Parks

There are beautiful State Parks all around our country, many with campgrounds. Find information in Woodall's Campground Guides or Google the state name and parks. One of the nicest places we have stayed was a state park in Florida called St. George Island State Park. Check it out at http://www.floridastateparks.org/stgeorgeisland/ . There is one at Lake Tawakoni in northeast Texas that is quite good. Go to http://www.tpwd.state.tx.us/state-parks/lake-tawakoni for more information on it.

City and County Parks

It's amazing how many nice little RV parks and campgrounds are tucked away in small towns around the country, especially in the Midwest. These hidden gems are usually found by word of mouth or in guidebooks to inexpensive camping. We find them by visiting the Chamber of Commerce in the area we are interested in. They have great information on camping as well as things to do and see in their area.

County Fairgrounds

When you travel the "US" highways and other red roads, you will see signs for county and even state fairgrounds. Most of these have camping of some kind. Often you will see an "honor box" to put money in for camping. Some of these even have fifty amp electric, water and sewer connections.

Corps of Engineers Parks

The U.S. Army Corps of Engineers maintain many recreation areas on or near their various projects. Go to http://www.usace.army.mil/Locations.aspx to find an area you might be interested in. Our friend Jane Kenny has written a book called "Corps Camping" which has just been revised. It is available from http://rvbookstore.com/ .

Casinos

Wouldn't you know it but Jane also wrote the definitive guide to Casino Camping. Now in its fifth revision, Casino Camping lists most of the casinos that allow RV parking or even have campgrounds adjacent to the casino itself. This book is also available from the good folks at http://rvbookstore.com/ . We have spent many nights at casinos. Some were simply parked in their lot with provision for RV's. We find out where the RV parking lot is located, and then we park with getting out easily in mind. Then we go into the casino for dinner and perhaps gaming.

One of our best casino camping experiences was at the Fire Lake Entertainment Center in Shawnee, OK. We had a fifty amp full hookup back-in site for eleven dollars a night. We made this our headquarters for exploring Oklahoma City.

Chapter 17 What About Boon docking?

Wikipedia, the free online encyclopedia, defines boondocks as: a remote, usually brushy rural area; or, a remote city or town that is considered unsophisticated. The expression was introduced to English by American military personnel serving in the Philippines during the early years of the 20th century. It derives from the Tagalog word "bundok", meaning "mountain". The term has evolved into American slang used to refer to the countryside or any implicitly isolated rural/wilderness area, regardless of topography or vegetation.

I prefer the definition given by Brian and Margie, owners of the website http://cheaprvliving.com/Boondocking.html . They outline boon docking as, "What is Boondocking? The RV community adopted the word to use it to describe remote camping in rural areas. So if you were going fishing in your truck camper to a remote National or State Park, when you got there you were camping in the boondocks. Since you had no hook-ups, but were self-sufficient, you were boon docking. Then some people noticed that while they were driving for several days to get to the boondocks, they could save some money by staying overnight in the parking lot of a WalMart. Since they had no hook-ups and were self-sufficient, they said they were boon docking. After a while people saw that they could save a lot of money by not staying in RV parks and so they started planning their trips around WalMart stores, staying in their parking lots most nights of their trip."

They go on to say "The term "boon docking" means different things to different people. Free camping, overnight RV parking at places such as WalMart or truck stops, and any time RV hookups are not available (dry camping) have been referred to as boon docking. http://www.rv-camping.org defines boon docking as remote location dispersed camping. With this in mind, you might call boon docking advanced RV camping. This type of camping isn't for everyone. Dispersed camping in remote areas requires research, exploration, and a sense of adventure to find great campsites."

While Kathy and I have only limited boon docking experience, we know many folks who do, and they have passed down some valuable information and tips for the would-be boon docker. We spent a week in Quartzite, AZ, camped with folks from our Escapee chapter. We were seven miles out of town, in the desert, within sight of at least five hundred other boonie lovers. That was lots of fun, and we will probably do it again sometime. We have also spent nights in parking lots at WalMart, Flying J, and other big box stores such as Cabela's and Bass Pro Shop when we were in travel mode. OK, it's soap-box time. We always look at the campgrounds in an area where we will stop. We call and get prices; if they are too expensive, we will consider a WalMart stop. WalMart is not a campground, although some may look like one in the evening. We stay one night only, no jacks down or slides out. We get permission from a manager and park where we are told to. Folks who stay for days with grills and awnings out can spoil this for all of us. Local campground owners shop at WalMart, too. They see the abuse and lobby the local city council for ordinances to stop overnight parking except in campgrounds. Enough said.

Almost all RVs have some self-containment features. There are holding tanks, propane gas appliances, battery banks, and generators. Add an inverter to your battery bank and you can use some AC powered appliances like TVs and computers. You will have almost all the comforts, for a while. Holding tanks aren't bottomless, batteries must be charged, and propane will eventually run out. "I've found this great wilderness campsite, so how do we stay for more than a few days?" I'm glad you asked. We'll start with holding tanks.

Water Conservation

Most of the fresh water making capacity on many Navy ships is dedicated to cooling engines and other machinery. A Navy shower is designed to conserve the fresh water supply. You would:

Step into the shower.

Turn the water on and wet yourself down.

Turn the water off, and soap up your body.

Step back into the shower.

Quickly rinse the soap off.

This is the most efficient use of your fresh water, and minimizes waste. There are aftermarket shower valves that completely shut off the flow. That way you can leave the mixing valve(s) where they are to resume the proper temperature.

Really intense boon Dockers will shower with a plastic dish pan on the floor of the shower stall. The water they collect is reused to flush the toilet.

While waiting for hot water to reach the faucet save water in a container and use it later for coffee or washing dishes.

Brush your teeth with water in a small cup and then rinse your mouth with another small cup of fresh water.

Wash dishes and utensils in small plastic tub to save water. Pour water outside if possible. Water the vegetation.

If you have long hair, wash your hair in a small plastic tub in the galley sink using one quart of water to wet hair and rinse. Then use about one quart fresh water for the final rinse.

Use a five gallon collapsible fresh water bottle to store extra water.

If your toilet cannot be flushed without activating the water valve, install a water cutoff valve in the supply line. This will allow the use of other methods or even the use of lake or creek water to flush with.

If your toilet has a sprayer use it to quickly rinse the toilet instead of holding down the foot pedal.

When possible use restrooms in stores, restaurants, service stations, etc., as well as in the campground if available.

Use disposable paper plates, bowls and cups, and plastic forks, spoons and knives.

Plan meals that are easy to make and clean-up. You might be able to live off pre-packaged meals that can just be reheated, and then the containers disposed of with no clean-up. If you hate frozen dinners, try to plan meals that might be cooked ahead of time that can be easily reheated on the stovetop, or in the microwave (using the generator).

Try to avoid using a lot of pots and dishes that will need to be washed.

Utilize wet wipes for minor boon docking cleaning chores of counters, hands, faces etc. to conserve water.

Buy a portable wheeled dumping container (Blue Boy) that you can tow behind a car to a dump station. With a couple of trips, you can extend the capacity of your black and grey tanks.

A water bladder is available that will fit in the back of an SUV and carry as much as forty to fifty gallons of water. Use a twelve volt pump to transfer the water to your fresh water tank. Just remember that water weighs about eight pounds per gallon.

We have a forty-five gallon black tank. The two of us can go two weeks before we have to dump it. You can extend this by putting used toilet paper in a sealed plastic bag. This will save some capacity in the black tank.

Electrical Conservation

Consider the purchase of a solar battery charging system. You must do the homework to decide how many solar panels will provide the power you need. Check out RV Solar Electric at http://www.rvsolarelectric.com/ , or the folks at AM Solar at http://amsolar.com/ . Be aware that almost every RV with batteries will have what is known as "phantom loads". These can be televisions and stereos that you leave plugged in, clocks, fans, control circuits in propane appliances, and even engine and transmission ECMs (electronic control modules). There are probably others we aren't aware of. Without solar charging, you must run your generator to maintain the charge on your house batteries. This can be expensive and bother any neighbors close by. Small wind turbines are just now becoming popular with RVers. Check the internet or boondocker on-line forums for more information on these.

Be realistic when you are using battery power. You absolutely cannot operate an air conditioner on battery power. Large draw appliances such as electric fry pans, toaster ovens and coffee makers will draw down your battery bank in a hurry. Probably the worst offender is the typical RV forced air furnace. "But it runs on propane", you say. The fan that moves the warm air and all the control electronics run on twelve volts and are a big draw-down.

Run your refrigerator and hot water heater on propane. Try to determine how much propane you use over time. This will tell you how long before you need more propane. You must plan your usage around the battery capacity you have. Of course, you might be able to add batteries to increase capacity. It's only money.

With a well-designed solar charging system, you should have enough battery power in the evening for lights and for the inverter to provide power to the TV, satellite dish, computer, cell phone and camera battery chargers, etc.

The move towards using Light Emitting Diodes (LED) to replace incandescent twelve volt lights in RVs is a win for the boon Docker. These lights operate with one tenth the current draw of conventional lamps. Now there are LED replacements for fluorescent lights as well. Here are some other energy saving tips:

Use only one light at a time and it should be the smallest light to do the job.

Limit use of large electrical loads like TVs, microwave and hair dryer.

Turn inverter off when not using it.

Turn off all 12 volt loads that are not being used - clock, radio, TV antenna booster, plug-in cubes for cell phones, printers, computers, etc.

Be sure to isolate large appliance AC circuits from your inverter. The draw from this equipment would empty the largest RV battery bank far faster than your solar array can recharge.

Older inverters operate on modified sine wave. However, many electronic devices, especially computers, require pure sine wave. Investigate what you need before you invest in your inverter. Pure sine wave inverters are widely available, they just cost more.

Consider several smaller inverters. They draw less current to power up the same appliance than a large two thousand watt inverter.

Inverters also will protect delicate electronics from power surges.

Inverters draw a small amount of power, even when there are no loads. Always switch them off when not in use.

Fantastic fans work with very low power draws, and move a lot of air.

Propane Conservation

Turn the water heater off until 10 or 15 minutes before you need hot water. Then, turn it off immediately. Turn it on again when you absolutely need hot water.

During cooler weather, close the bedroom door at night to keep the bedroom warmer. This will save propane.

Consider the purchase of a catalytic heater to keep you warm. They are very fuel efficient and use no power. Be sure to open a small vent to prevent both condensation in your rig and carbon monoxide poisoning.

General RV Boondocking Tips

Orient your RV to maximize cooling or heating depending on your need. Maximize the sun through the windows for heat or make the shade of the awnings most effective for cooling. Orient for cross ventilation of breezes as well.

Keep the bumper stickers on your rig to a minimum. You may be proud of your NRA membership, but the thieves working the parking lot see that sticker as the likelihood of high value property.

Don't just turn off the "Blue" road and take off blind down a narrow dirt road! You may find out there isn't a campsite and worse yet, you can't turn around. You may want to stay in a campground for a night or two while you scout the area in your tow vehicle.

Take your trash to town. Do not leave it, burned in a campfire. Properly dispose of it in an appropriate dumpster. Seek permission of a company or store which you patronized, or use a public dumpster

Boondocking Publications

Check out http://www.hitchitch.com/ for a source of RV and Boondocking tips.

Shunpiker's Guides to RV Boon docking http://www.frugal-rv-travel.com/

The Complete Book of Boondock RV'ing: Camping Off the Beaten Path by Bill and Jan Moeller

BOONDOCKING: Finding a Perfect Campsite on America's Public Lands by Bob Difley

Chapter 18 Working on the Road

To quote from the home page of Workamper News, "Workampers are adventurous individuals, couples and families who have chosen a wonderful lifestyle that combines any kind of part-time or full-time work with RV camping. If you work as an employee, operate a business, or donate your time as a volunteer, and you sleep in an RV (or on-site housing), you are a Workamper!"

Do you want to RV but need a little extra income? Well, we are in the same boat. Or, you may want to do volunteer work. There are enough opportunities to work and volunteer out here on the road that we don't see any unemployment problems. Many folks have left a lifetime of work and in retirement, want to give back something. There is a world of volunteer opportunities available to them. You may want to be on the road full time but need some additional income. There are many, many paying jobs you may have never thought about. Lots of RVers are willing to trade a few hours of work for a campsite in an area they wish to visit. We have done all of this, and we are the richer for it.

In our first year RVing, we joined an Escapee group of Red Cross Disaster Volunteers. Almost immediately after training, we found ourselves in San Antonio, TX, working in a shelter for victims of Hurricanes Katrina and Rita. That was an amazing three weeks. We also did two stints of volunteer work at the Escapee CARE (Continuing Assistance for Retired Escapees) Center in Livingston, TX. I've never washed so many pots and dishes, and at the same time been so happy about it in my life.

We have also worked in campgrounds across the country, both for a campsite and for campsite and money. These jobs were easy for us to find, and you can, too. There are, however, some basic principles to remember when you decide to work as part of your RV lifestyle. The main thing is: you are not starting a new career. These are part-time seasonal jobs. The pay, if any, will be at or near minimum wage. Secondly, unless you have been hired as a manager, do not try to be one. This can quickly lead to problems between you and management, and can just as quickly lead to dismissal. If you can keep these basics in mind, and keep a good work ethic and attitude; you will be successful.

Volunteering

Many of the volunteer opportunities for RVers are with Federal, State, and local government agencies. Check out http://www.volunteer.gov/gov/ . You can search for positions by state, zip code, and by the type of job you would like to do. Most of these jobs will not include an RV site. Type RV Site in the keyword box for those. Make sure you are in agreement with all the requirements of the position you want. Better to decline now than to make a commitment and drive a thousand miles only to find out you don't like the job. We know a few folks who love to volunteer at various fish hatcheries. Another volunteer job involves setting up a spotting telescope to help tourists to observe wildlife. We have met several volunteer docents at Pacific Coast lighthouses who come back year after year. Having an RV site perched atop a bluff overlooking the Pacific Ocean in Oregon might be part of the reason. How cool would it be to live and work at your favorite National Park like Yellowstone, or Glacier? Some of the National Parks even have paid positions.

The Escapees RV Club has two particularly outstanding volunteer opportunities for Escapees members. They are:

Continuing Assistance for Retired Escapees (CARE) was mentioned previously. Volunteers here help operate the facility by cooking and cleaning up after meals, driving participants to doctor's appointments and shopping, and being on-call during staff off hours.

Disaster Operations Volunteer Escapees (DOVE) was also mentioned earlier. After provided training, DOVE volunteers participate in Red Cross disaster operations when and where they may occur.

Numerous church denominations have volunteer organizations that participate in building and maintaining churches and church properties. Some are:

USMAPS (Assembly of God Mission America Placement Service) USMAPS was formed to **help** meet the need for construction and renovation of churches, Assemblies of God colleges and universities, and other facilities. Another goal is to **strengthen** the arm of evangelism of U.S. Missions ministries by encouraging and facilitating non-construction RVers and church teams' involvement with U.S. Missions evangelism outreaches. http://usmaps.ag.org/

SOWER (Servants on Wheels Ever Ready) this ministry is primarily a physical labor ministry. While there is an occasional need for office-type work, on most projects the men are involved with the construction or remodeling of structures and associated utilities, repair of vehicles, or landscape installation using their skills in carpentry, electrical, plumbing, roofing, masonry, mechanics, etc. Women have helped with office work, tutoring, sewing, painting, kitchen work, cleaning, etc. There are opportunities for everyone of reasonably good health to contribute. http://www.sowerministry.org/

NOMADS (Nomads on a Mission Active in Divine Service) provide volunteer labor for United Methodist organizations. NOMADS demonstrate God's love through our work and by listening to the people with whom we work. They do new construction, remodeling, and repairs for churches, children's homes, camps, colleges, outreach missions and disaster rebuilding. Team members do maintenance, cleaning, painting, electrical, drywall, sewing, and flooring. http://www.nomadsumc.org/

Another type of volunteer job is with various charitable organizations. These might include:

RV Care-A-Vanners is a volunteer program for anyone who travels in a recreational vehicle, wants to build Habitat for Humanity houses, and have fun doing it. RV Care-A-Vanners welcomes people of all ages, from all walks of life who want to pick up a hammer and help change lives. http://www.habitat.org/rv/

The Good Sam Club has many non-profit volunteer possibilities with other likeminded RVers.

Workamping
Workamping typically means trading your labor for an RV site. The electricity may or may not be included. This type of job is usually in a campground in one of their departments. You could work in the office, maintenance, grounds, food service, security, or perhaps in the activities department. These are quite typical jobs that RVers

may take. You should receive your site and utilities for perhaps ten hours of work each, or maybe a little more. You may not be asked to do any more than that; or you may be asked to work more hours for pay (usually minimum wage for the state). This is how the bulk of workamping jobs are offered. Some places will offer pay for all hours worked but you pay a discounted rate for your site. Many high end resorts do this. You might even be fortunate enough to find work where you are paid for all hours and receive a free site. There are many other types of jobs out there for RVers.

You might work at an amusement park such as Adventure Land in Iowa where they have a campground for workampers. Maybe you want to work at Disney World? They do not have housing for you, but you will receive passes to the park for your family. You could work at Dollywood in Tennessee and get health insurance while you are working.

Most of this type of job requires a seasonal commitment. This means the whole summer or winter season. Some positions even offer an end-of-season bonus for staying to the end. If you don't want to commit so much time, consider something like the sugar beet harvest in North Dakota. It lasts between two and four weeks and pays quite well. Maybe you have the stamina to work for Amazon.com in one of their warehouses for the eight to twelve weeks leading up to Christmas? This job could require you to walk as much as fifteen miles a day while lifting heavy packages. They do not have campgrounds for you. You have to find your own.

I've just scratched the surface of the different possibilities available to you. My best advice is to go to workamper.com http://www.workamper.com/ and sign up with them. For a very reasonable fee, you will have access to their Awesome Applicants resume database. Once you complete your resume there, it will be made available to employers signed up with Workamper. Kathy and I have found all but one of our jobs through their service. We receive e-mail daily with new job postings. We submitted resumes to those employers we wanted to work for, and sometimes we received multiple offers and got to pick and choose. That's a good situation to be in.

Other sources for workamping jobs are:

http://www.happyvagabonds.com/

http://www.work-camping.com/

http://www.workampingjobs.com/

http://www.work-for-rvers-and-campers.com/

Workamper.com

One of the best places we have found is Workamper.com. It is where we have gotten most of our jobs, and we have found them to have all kinds of information on their web site. They have quite a bit of advice for those just starting out working on the road. Their resume database is scanned by many, many prospective employers. A bi-monthly magazine, the Workamper News, contains job listings in every state as well as general information. Daily e-mail notices of newly posted jobs are available as an option. We support Workamper.com because they provide complete service for the workamper. As such we occupy a Concierge position with them which allows us to offer a free issue of the magazine if you join through the posting on our website: http://www.livingthervdream.com/ . Otherwise, please use the code hugg4019 in the "referred by" space on the application. We are compensated by Workamper.com for generating new members.

Workamping Tips

We were able to interview the manager at our last campground job and there is some real gold in this interview from the perspective of the employer. They had worked very hard at selecting their workcamping team, and they looked at over 5000 applications. Here are some of the thoughts that they had and what they are looking for:

They look though a lot of resumes and the first important thing is the introduction to your resume. Make it eye catching, not just: we are John and Kathy, but we are full of life, and we are friendly and outgoing. We are people persons.

Don't concentrate on what you did before you retired unless it would pertain to the job you are applying for at the campground.

If you have workamped before, put that at the top of the resume

Did you work with a specific campground reservation system? Which one?

Specify if you have a special skill such as builder, office work, electrician, or anything that will pertain to the position you are applying for.

You should bold the specific skills you have such as **campground master, or CPO** certificate.

Demonstrate good people skills. This will help catch the eye of the manager.

Because managers have so many resumes to look at, it's good to have a bullet list of your skills and the talents that you have. It makes it a whole lot easier for the manager to pull out your resume and look it over. Don't forget: if you are looking for an office job and have a lot of spelling errors, it will not help you. Use spell check.

If you use the phrase "open to all possibilities," then make sure you are. It will get you through the first group of reviews.

The average manager will look at thousands of resumes every year - you will want yours to jump out at him or her.

If you are looking for a paid position, do not apply where pay is not being offered. It is a waste of time for you and for the manager. Read the posting and make sure it offers everything that you are looking for. Don't throw out your resume to the world hoping that if you don't get a paying job, you will take one that doesn't. It's not fair to the hiring manager or to you.

Employers are registered with workcamper.com and they can put in key words to bring up resumes that would fit the positions that they have available. Use the words that are in the posting for this reason.

Keep your resume up to date. Revise it every six months to be sure it is current. There is nothing more frustrating than having to look at a resume that is 10 years old. If you are looking for a job in the northwest, put that in there so those campgrounds looking for workers will know that you will be a good fit.

Get a commitment from the employer as to the particulars of the work in writing, and give a written commitment back to the employer.

Don't take the first job that comes along just to have a job. You will most likely be disappointed.

If you are looking for work, talk with the manager at the park you are interested in, and talk with the other workampers. Network and talk to people.

OK, you have been offered a job and you have arrived at the campground. What are the managers looking for now?

They expect you to be both on time and who you have claimed to be. If you said you know Campground Master and you don't, then you have lied.

You are not the only new employee. There may be as many as 200 or as few as 2 and everyone needs to be brought up to speed on all the systems and how that particular campground uses them.

Download the reservation program used in the campground and practice if it has been a while since you have used it. Then you can relax and enjoy the experience.

Once you have been hired, change your status to not available until the next season if you use the Awesome Applicants feature at Workamper.com.

Here is some more good advice that came out of that interview:

If you need experience, go to the park during the off season. The managers will have time to work with you, and you will have time to learn and become an asset to the campground.

Work on the cleaning crew and take an hour or two on your own time to learn how to work in the office.

Be honest about your physical abilities; if you are unable to do outside work anymore, learn how to do office work. There is no reason a man can't work in the office or a woman can't do maintenance work.

Employers are looking for friendly and outgoing people. They want the park's reputation to be that of a friendly and clean park.

Make sure the pictures on your resume are up to date.

Workamper.com offers a class to help you write a resume. Remember, this is not a regular job; it is a seasonal part-time job, not a career.

If you need to make money, be sure to express this up front.

Make all your desires known. You might not get everything you want, but ask.

Do not print your resume in blue text. It is hard on the eyes.

Put info the employer wants up front. These are the things specified in the ad posting.

Keep it short; 1 page is more than adequate.

Give them something to remember. A short memorable story about you will be remembered years later.

Understand the area you are going to. If fly fishing is your thing, don't apply for a job in Arizona where lakes and streams are scarce. If surfing is your thing, there are plenty of jobs near the California coast. Go where there are opportunities to enjoy your particular interest.

Here are some books on working on the road that might be helpful:

Roadwork II: The RVers Ultimate Income Resource Guide by Arline Chandler

Support Your RV Lifestyle! With CD by Jaimie Hall Bruzenak

Work Your Way Across the USA by Nick Russell

Chapter 19 How do I Pick and Setup a Campsite?

We have tried to give you the reader the basics as well as wisdom from many of our RVing friends on site selection.

Site Selection

The first thing you need to determine is whether you need a pull-through or a back-in site. Many parks do not have pull-through sites, while some have them exclusively. Some parks that have both types will charge more for a pull-through than a back-in. For us, a pull-through site makes sense when we are traveling and only need a place to stop and sleep. When this is the case, we don't put out the slide or deploy the leveling jacks. We don't use any hook-ups except electric. We even leave the car hooked up. If we plan to stay in a place for several days or more, we will use a back-in site and set up our rig for comfort.

No matter what type of site you choose, do not pull in or back in until you have walked on the site. It should have adequate utilities such as thirty or fifty amp power. You should carry and use an AC outlet circuit tester that detects faulty wiring in 3-wire receptacles. These are small inexpensive devices that will detect reversed polarity and other conditions. With the appropriate adaptors, it will test a thirty Amp campground outlet at the pedestal. Once you know the power is correct, make sure your power cable will reach the pedestal. If you need a sewer connection, it should be close enough so you can reach it with the hose you carry. Is the hose bib or fresh water connection high enough off the ground to allow you to connect your water pressure regulator? These are basics and should be checked first. If there are problems, ask for another site.

Next you need to look up to verify that overhanging trees will not touch your rig and cause paint scratches or worse. Is the approach to the site and the front opening wide enough to accommodate your rig? Are there trees or other obstructions in your path?

Last but certainly not least is the matter of level. Is the site relatively level front to back and side to side? Will you need to use your whole lumberyard of bits and scraps of wood to make your rig level? Remember, your RV refrigerator will not work properly when it is not level to within a degree or two. We use a four foot carpenter's level to determine the final positioning so we can manually adjust our leveling jacks. If you have a trailer, purchase two inexpensive bubble levels so you can see how much to adjust.

Parking

OK, I did everything you said, and I'm on my way into the site. What next? I'm glad you asked. Parking an RV of any kind in a site requires precision maneuvering. This is where you and your partner need to get together on signals you both know and agree on. If you are outside the rig directing your partner, please do not have a dog in each arm and a cigarette in your mouth. I have seen this very thing; it was funny at first, but then it was just plain pitiful. Don't have any distractions when you are directing the parking of your home. Mistakes can be quite expensive. Friendly people will come up to you while you are parking and try to help. You must figure out how to tactfully tell them that you would rather do it the way you have practiced.

These same people will be there when you are unhooking your car from a motor home, or your truck from your trailer. If you let them, they will distract you to the point that you will forget a step and pay the price later. Tell them you will be happy to talk with them after you are parked and hooked up. The key thing to remember is to place the rig close enough to the utilities, but far enough away so basement doors will open. Some sites are built with the electric and the water and sewer split apart. Try to get in a place where your power cables and sewer hose will reach. This is when prior practice pays off. You should get several rubber parking cones and practice backing up in a large vacant parking lot. Churches are great places to do this if you can get permission. Keep it up until you both can agree on hand signals. Some folks use cell phones or walkie-talkies to communicate. If that works for you, go for it. Just remember, the driver needs to know whether you are directing the front or the rear of the rig, especially when backing trailers. This is a good time to mention that no matter how good a driver you think you are, it's better to have an outside observer to direct you. Otherwise, sudden, embarrassing, and expensive accidents can happen. We know from painful experience.

Site Setup

Congratulations, you made it into your site! There is just a little more work to do and you're ready to enjoy yourselves. No matter whether you have leveling jacks or scissor jacks, you should have jack pads under them. This keeps them from digging into the ground and protects the bottom of the jacks. There are many products on the market to do this. I made mine from a fourteen foot piece of weather treated two by twelve inch board. I had the store saw the board into one foot lengths and took them home. Then I laid two of them together with the grain running at right angles to one another and screwed them together with three inch galvanized screws. I also purchased six screw-in eye bolts. I put an eye bolt in each assembly to make it easy to reach with an awning rod. We store these in milk crates and use them as both jack pads and drive on leveling pads. Sometimes you just can't get a level site. We also have two sets of plastic leveling blocks. With all that, we can level almost anywhere.

Now we'll hook up the umbilical connections for power, water, sewer, and cable TV if available. Use your AC circuit tester on the power pedestal to make sure there are no problems before you plug in your rig. Turn the breaker(s) off before plugging in. Then turn on the breaker. Be sure to hook up your water pressure regulator first and then the shortest length of water hose that will reach. Turn on the water and check for leaks. The RV park may require a rubber doughnut to seal the sewer connection. They may also require the sewer hose be suspended off the ground. These are probably dictated by local laws and ordinances. This is a good time to remind you to have disposable rubber gloves on hand, (literally). Unless you have a full black and/or grey tank, it is best to leave your sewer valves closed until you need to dump. If cable TV is available, hook this up as well. It's a good idea to have two twenty five foot lengths of TV cable and a female to female adaptor to use both together.

Now it's time to get the ladder down if you have sunscreens to hang on the windshield. It might be a good idea to clean the windshield first so you don't have to do it when you're getting ready to hit the road again.

From here on out, your personal tastes determine how you fix up your campsite. You will probably want a patio mat or other kind of ground covering in front of the entrance door. An awning tie-down kit will help on some windy days. Lights, lawn ornaments, flags, personal signs and who knows what else will finish up your site. A visit to Camping World will give you some great ideas on this.

Chapter 20 How About RVing with Pets?

Do you already have a pet, or are you considering getting a pet? It's an important decision to make. You must consider just what kind of pet(s) you have, how they will travel with you, and how you will care for them. We have seen people traveling with dogs, cats, birds, and even heard of someone who has snakes (not my favorite); but whatever you now have, it takes some consideration to travel with your pet. Not every dog or cat enjoys traveling.

There are new laws coming that may require that your pet be restrained or buckled up when traveling. We think a cage with plenty of room inside is probably the best way for both you and your pet(s) to travel. Make sure the cage is secured so it won't fly around if you have to stop quickly.

What is the right pet for you? If you are looking for one, consider whether you have any allergies or if you have a strong preference for one type or another. Make sure your current pet will be able to travel comfortably. If not, there may be a lot of friction, and neither one of you will enjoy the experience. Do not take a pet with you unless you have strong feeling towards him or her. Does your pet have a great personality? Does it like traveling? Size is a big consideration. Two seems to be the limit at most RV parks. Some parks are very strict, and some are lenient. You don't want to be asked to leave a park because of your pets. What about special needs for your pet? Can you get the special food or the right medication for them while traveling? If you leave your pet in your RV for any length of time, consider having an automatic generator start installed. That way, if the power goes out, as happens when it is very hot, your pet will have air conditioning and stay healthy.

Cats tend to be very independent and do not bark, so they could be easily left in the air-conditioned RV while you are out exploring. They do however, need a litter box, although I have seen cats being walked on a leash. That was an eye opener. Where will you put the litter box? Some have used the shower stall for the litter box and go to the bathhouse at the park. What will be your solution? Ask yourself these questions before you travel, or before you buy your RV and obtain a cat.

Dogs are easily accommodated in most RVs and RV parks. There may be some restrictions on the breed or size of the dogs. When you call for a reservation be sure to let them know you have a pet, what kind, and how much it weighs. When you check in, bring your vaccination records with you. It just saves time. I have only had 2-3 parks ask for the records, but it shows the manager of the park you are a responsible pet owner. Some dogs get anxious when you are not with them and will bark a lot. This is very inconsiderate to your neighbors, and it is important to keep everything friendly at the park. Bring your dog's kennel or bed and it will help with the adjustment to camp life. It will be a little taste of home for your pet. While actually traveling, it will help keep your pet safe. Grooming can be another issue. Does your pet need to be groomed, and where will you have it done? We have found that by talking to fellow RVers in the park, they will recommend a good groomer, or they will let us know if the local one is not so good. We found a great groomer in Benson, AZ, that only charged $25.00, and a pet center that charges $65.00. So, ask around to get the best one for you and your pet. Usually the park employees can also recommend someone to take care of your pet, whether you need grooming or veterinary care. Ask around before you have the need of one of these professionals.

There are many dogs and cats at your local shelter, so please consider getting an older pet from one of the local shelters. All of our dogs have been found at the local shelters, and they have been a real blessing to us.

Park Pet Rules

Keep your pet on a leash at all times. No matter how good your pet is, they may see some other dog or person and take off after it for no real reason. Even the best trained pet may bolt for no apparent reason. I have had this happen twice in parks. Both times, it really scared me. I was just walking my dog, and a German Sheppard was off leash in an open field, being trained. He took one look and me and my dog, and came after us. Fortunately I turned my shoulder and he did not injure either of us. That owner threw the dog in his rig and was packed up and out of the park in about 5 minutes. I was so shocked by the whole thing I didn't report the incident. The next time, as I was walking my dog, I saw an owner who had two standard poodles off leash; when I mentioned that the dogs should be on a leash, she said that that was not a problem because her dogs never left her side. So, as I was returning from my walk and passing her RV, those two dogs came running at full speed up to me and were jumping all over me. I know they meant no harm, but it was a very unpleasant experience, especially since the first incident really frightened me. Please keep them on their leash.

Do not allow your pet to continually be barking all the time. It is so unpleasant to try and have a meal outside or to be sitting outside just enjoying the evening and there in the next camping spot is this aggressive barking, growling, and snarling dog.

Do not leave your pet unattended for long periods of time. Dogs get bored when left alone for long periods of time and they start barking and becoming a nuisance. We leave the TV on or you could leave a radio playing. It gives the dog some sense of comfort, and makes them feel like they are not alone.

Always pick up after your pet. You would not like to step in poop, so don't leave your dog's poop for others to step in. We keep plastic grocery bags and use them as a poop bag. Some parks will have a dog run and will have bags you can use. Please don't take a whole bunch of bags, they are for everyone to use. Leave some for others. It is so nice of the parks to supply these bags, don't abuse the privilege.

Here's the Scoop on the Poop

Microorganisms like whipworm, roundworm, hookworm, parvo and coccidian thrive in your dog's poop. If the poop isn't picked up and disposed of properly, these organisms can infect the land and water, causing sickness and infections. People and pets can be affected by storm water that has been contaminated, and at some beaches the rise in bacteria levels are so high that everyone must stay out of the water. Fines for not picking up the poop can range from $100 to over $750; over 3.6 billion pounds of dog poop are produced in the United States every year. I have no idea who or how they measured this. A single gram of dog waste can contain 23 million fecal coli form bacteria. It's a simple process to pick it up. Get a plastic bag, bend over and pick it up, then tie it up and put it in the trash. I always carry two bags just in case he does a double duty. Campgrounds are becoming so fed up with pet owners who do not pick up after their pets that some are no longer allowing any pets in their parks. Do your duty, and pick up after your pet.

Make sure you have some kind of ID, whether it is a tag, microchip, or a photo of your pet. They can easily get lost or forgotten. I know you are saying, "I would never leave my pet." Well, we were in a park and found this really cute Shih-Tzu up by the front office. The owners have 3 of them and thought all of them were in the fifth wheel. They had already left the park. Fortunately there was a tag on the dog, and we were able to call the owners before they were too far down the road. The dog had slipped out the door as the couple was unhooking their rig; they pulled out, thinking all the dogs were in the rig.

Bring all of your records with you, in case your pet becomes ill on the road. The emergency vet you will see knows that at the last check-up your pet was okay. Also, having the shot records is a huge help because the vet will be able to rule out some things and get right to the heart of the problem. Also, you will need this information when you are crossing the borders into and out of the United States. When crossing the borders, be sure to have the receipt of where you purchased your pet food with you. Coming back to the United States, all pet food from Canada is prohibited because of Mad Cow disease. So, if you have Canadian food just donate it to a shelter and get new as soon as you cross the border. Also, when crossing into Canada, some pet foods containing meat products (even in cans) are not allowed.

Dangerous Dogs

The old rule that a dog is allowed one bite is no longer true. One study found that a dog bite can cause the owner over $16,000.00 in penalties. It's no fun for the owner or people around you to be worried about your dog biting someone. Maybe now is not the time to start RVing if you have a dog with this problem. Campsites are much closer together than homes. Some cities have banned certain breeds. You know you have a great pet, but the city does not; they may have had trouble with pets of that same breed. So be sure that the park you want to go to has no restriction, or if they do, what are they? It would not to fun to pull into a park and be turned away because of the breed of pet you have is restricted in the city or county.

We love having Charlie with us. He's a 10 pound Poodle and Bischon mix and what a joy; but there are times, especially when it is raining, that I wonder: is this a good idea? Going out in the thunderstorms to walk the dog can be unpleasant, but the joy of having him in our lives far outweighs that. He also has given us an excuse to meet people. If you have a friendly, well behaved animal, people love to come and pet them; then there's a chance to make a new friend. We were just in a park with a Poodle and a Bischon, and Charlie is a mix of the two. It was fun to watch them run and play together. But, we have been in parks that had pets running loose and have become a real nuisance to everyone's enjoyment of the campground. We have seen people kicked out of parks because they did not pick up after their pet, or the pet had become such a nuisance that the park could not allow them to remain. So, choose your pet wisely, and take care of their training and medical needs.

Chapter 21 How Can You Stay Fit On The Road?

Well, you bought the RV, sold the house and stuff, and you are now on the road to adventure. However, now you seem to have more time on your hands. It only takes a short time to totally clean the RV and you are wondering what to do next? This can cause you to get very lazy. It's so easy to start the day with a cup of coffee outside and watch everyone getting up and starting their day; there may even be some wildlife giving you morning entertainment. WOW, what a life; but you still want to stay healthy and active, and this will require some planning. Every day it is so important to do something. Walk, ride your bike, hike, jog, swim, jump rope, dance, or do yoga. Being active is a necessity; some authorities recommend 30 minutes, 3 times a week, to maintain your health.

This doesn't seem like much, but with so much to do and so much to see, planning is essential. I like to get up and take a walk every morning. I am usually up by 6AM - the campground is quiet, and the sun is coming up. What a great time of the day! However, if I don't get it done *then*, I don't seem to get it done at all. I have seen campers doing yoga in the morning sun, riding bikes, riding a stationary bike, lifting weights, jumping rope, swimming laps, roller blading, and jogging. What will work for you? If you don't like to be outdoors, try exercise videos. Maybe going for a hike will fill the need? Parks will usually have a list of hikes in the local area, and they are rated easy, medium, and strenuous. The National Parks are great for this; the newspaper you get when you enter will list all the hikes, rate them and then give a description of what is involved. The trail might be 3.2 miles round trip with a rise in elevation of 250ft. Campgrounds will also have a walk laid out around the campground, so you can judge the distance and keep a record if you want. They can also recommend local hikes, and state and city parks that will fit the bill. If you are not in good shape, check with your doctor first to make sure it is okay to start some kind of program.

When I first started walking 40 years ago, the best I could do was to walk down the drive-way and go one house down; but I kept at it, and each week would add one more house. Then, I started adding blocks. Today, it is easy for me to walk 3-4 miles a day. Just get started, and every week add a little more. You will feel better, and if you have a partner with you, the walk is a great chance to spend quality time together. Talk about your plans for the day, or talk about the day you had together. As you can see I love to walk, but you can find something else to do no matter what it is; as Nike says "just do it."

Eating right is really easy. Although the kitchen area is small, there is still plenty of room to prepare food. Farmers markets may be close, and since you have time, enjoy the wonders of farmers markets. Different areas of the country have different specialties. Eastern Washington State has an abundance of wonderful fresh fruits and vegetables, corn on the cob in the Midwest, tomatoes almost anywhere, and fresh shrimp along the Gulf coast. Just take a few minutes, ask and look around, and you will find everything you need to have a healthy and delicious meal. There are many wonderful cookbooks just for RVers, and going online to find a great recipe is fun. I just put in the ingredients that I have on hand, and several great meals will come up. I like the ones that recommend barbequing. That's John's job, so I can just sit and watch. If you have a special diet, make sure that what you need is available in the area you will be in, or if possible, order it online. Most campgrounds will accept UPS or FedEx deliveries; just be sure and ask before you have anything sent to the campground. Stock your RV with single serving healthy snacks, so you are not tempted to get fast food. If you do stop for fast food, try the salads or the healthier version rather than the same old hamburger. Remember, when you are in travel mode: be sure to stop every couple of hours, get out and stretch. We go with the 3,3,3 plan: no more than 300 miles a day, stop every 3 hours to stretch, and stay at least 3 days. Of course this is the plan, sometimes it's more, and sometimes it's less. And last but not least, make sure you get plenty of rest. We try to get at least 6-8 hours a night. I don't know about you, but I get cranky when I am tired. A little planning will make the full-timing adventure fun and exciting. Keeping fit will help the adventure to last longer and be much more enjoyable. See you on the trails!

Chapter 22 What about Rig Maintenance?

Let's face it, you have made a major investment in your rig, and you will want it to give you many years of fun. Routine preventive maintenance will help to ensure that. Since Kathy and I full-time, we are doing maintenance constantly. Some of you may have to store your rig for a season and I'll touch a little on that. The first maintenance thing I did when we bought the rig was to purchase a Maintenance Log. It was a general purpose book for all types of rigs, but all the pertinent stuff for our diesel pusher motor home was there. I lined out the stuff that didn't fit.

I compared all the maintenance entries with the information in all the service manuals that came with the rig. If you do not have these, you can obtain them from the manufacturers of all the various appliances and other items that are in your rig. I got quite a few from websites with downloadable documents. The rig manual can be obtained from the rig manufacturer. Also make sure you have engine and transmission maintenance data from those manufacturers. If your manufacturer is no longer in business, try the Forum section on http://www.rv.net .

Next, I set up my maintenance log in accordance with the information I found in the manuals. Then I had to decide what preventive maintenance steps I could accomplish myself and what needed to be done by professionals. Anything having to do with engine, transmission, and brakes was left to either Freightliner, the chassis maker, or Cummins Engine, the engine maker. Fortunately, there are service centers across the country that can handle maintenance on almost every make of RV.

We change engine oil every five thousand miles or yearly, whatever comes first. Included with that service is a thorough chassis lubrication and replacement of oil and fuel filters. Make sure whoever does your work will follow exactly the manufacturer's guidelines. You don't want them to skip any steps. Explain what you want and get them to put it in writing on the service ticket. We usually have the generator's oil and filter changed at that time as well.

On diesel rigs with air brakes, there are replaceable air dryer filters that must be replaced periodically. Allison automatic transmissions are on most diesel rigs, and they need filters and transmission fluid changed periodically. Although I could probably do the generator maintenance myself, it's just too easy to let the professionals do it along with the engine maintenance.

Such obvious things as; oil changes, fuel filter changes, lubrication requirements, tire air checks, fridge service checks, furnace checks, AC checks, battery checks, water heater checks, and on and on.

Any of these items listed above can cause you a lot of heartache while traveling if they stop working properly, so you really need to see that they are in good shape before your trip.

If you store your rig for a season and then plan to use it for a long trip, schedule all the preventive maintenance at least a few weeks before you want to depart. Problems can appear and parts will have to be ordered. I believe you should give the drive train and brake system first priority, along with tire checking and battery charging. Those are the things that get you there. Next, complete the maintenance steps for your appliances and other systems. Plan ahead and you will depart on time with peace of mind that your rig has all maintenance done.

These are the other things that will need periodic preventive maintenance. Get it done before a big trip so you won't have to scramble for a repair shop in an unfamiliar town.

There are some RV system items that might be better left to a qualified mechanic. These are mostly propane fired appliances. Now you are looking at the possibility of a fire. Some of the maintenance steps can be done by a handy RV owner, but doing other required steps to determine LP gas pressure and leaks require expensive, specialized equipment. Those steps should not be skipped. These appliances include the following:

Refrigerator - The owner's manual has a simple list of items that the owner can do, but there are others that should be done by a certified technician.

Furnace(s) - You don't want it to stop working in the middle of a freak cold snap because all the proper steps of the maintenance were not done. Leave this maintenance to the pros.

Hot Water Heater - I have spent more than a few hours working on our hot water heater. I have cleaned the tank of calcium crystal growth from heating hard water. I have replaced the electric heating element twice. I've replaced the inlet and outlet hoses because the original ones had cheap plastic connectors that broke and caused floods in the bedroom. What fun that was in the middle of the night. I leave anything having to do with the gas system to the pros.

Air Conditioner(s) – The primary user maintenance for RV air conditioners is to keep the filter clean. These can be removed and washed with warm water. This should be done every two weeks during the AC season. If you are comfortable up on your roof, remove the shroud or large fiberglass cover and check the pan for moisture. If there is standing water, clear the drain holes. Check between the cooling fins and the fan for leaves and other debris. This should be removed with compressed air. Clean the evaporator coils with a soft brush. Inspect, clean, and straighten any bent condenser fins on the unit. Use a knife or any other thin and sturdy metal edge. The cooling system is sealed. Leave that to the pros!

Batteries - Battery cables should be intact, and the connectors kept tight at all times. Always use insulated tools to avoid shorting battery terminals. Clean the terminals and cable end connectors with a water and baking soda solution. Use a stiff brush and clean until shiny and the green is gone. Make sure the entire top of the battery is clean and free of dirt and corrosion. Always use distilled water to replenish batteries. Check batteries at least monthly, more often in the hot summer. You may find that it is difficult to open the battery covers because of all the heavy wiring on top of the batteries. We use a battery watering system called "Pro-Fil" we found at Camping World. It consists of new cell top covers that form a water manifold that will water all your house batteries at one time. A small bulb siphon pump brings the distilled water from its container and into the manifold. When the bulb is too hard to squeeze, all cells are at the proper level. We have all four of our six volt house batteries hooked up with this system. This is also available for twelve volt batteries. Too easy!

Wiper Blades – Operate the wipers often. If there are constant streaks, replace them with new units of the same length. Also exercise the windshield washers. Replace the hoses if needed. The openings can be cleared with a needle.

Window & Slide Seals & Gaskets – Check the window and slide-out gaskets and seals. They should be lubricated with a silicone based spray twice a year to assure that they remain pliable and do not dry out and crack.

Slide-out mechanisms – Check your owner's manual for maintenance steps for your slides. Ours has a rack and matching gear at each end. Both should be lubricated according to the manufacturer's specifications. While you're at it, check the manual slide in and out system for proper operation. You will need it at the worst possible time like at night and or in the rain. I'm just sayin'.

Leveling Jacks – Like the slide system, the jacks must be lubricated in accordance with the maker's specifications. Ours are hydraulic, and have grease fittings on each jack. The shiny part of the cylinder should be sprayed with a silicone based spray as well. I also check the hydraulic fluid level in the tank every two months. Some other systems are electric and have different requirements.

Roof – Let's face it, the roof is what keeps you dry when it rains. Older rigs may have a metal, or aluminum roof. Later model rigs will have a roof covering made of either fiberglass or rubber, also known as EPDM (you don't want to know what this is short for). Primary maintenance for all is to keep them clean and inspect the seals and gaskets of the roof mounted stuff like air conditioners, vents, antennas, and sewer vents. We clean our roof four times a year and more often if we have been parked under trees dripping sap and other nasty stuff. Pay special attention to the area where the front and rear fiberglass caps are joined. If you find cracking or deterioration in the seals, clean the area and add sealant material on and around the area.

EPDM roofs require some special care. Never clean them with a petroleum or citrus based cleaner as it will harm the EPDM material. There are many cleaners on the market specifically designed for rubber roofs. The chalking or streaking you see is a normal part of the aging process for this material. Look carefully for cuts or tears in the rubber membrane that will cause leaking. Repair with special EPDM repair material available in RV supply stores like Camping World.

Emergency Exit – Every RV has an emergency exit besides the main door. Exercise this at least monthly, and lubricate it as needed to ensure it will open smoothly when you really need it. If it is a window like ours, cut and notch a piece of wood to hold it open.

Otherwise, it will slam on your hand or fingers to add to the stress of going out of your window during an emergency.

Tires - Inspect your tires, the sidewalls in particular. Unfortunately, you should look at the inside surfaces too. This is not fun on rear dual tires, but an inspection mirror and a flashlight will help. Check for cracks and cuts. A cut on the open road can lead to a blowout. Cracks in the sidewall are a sign of dry rot. If you find signs of dry rot, plan on replacing all the rig's tires.

Next, you must check air pressure in all the tires, both rig and towed vehicle, or truck and trailer. Get a good quality air gauge that can handle the pressure required in your tires. It is best to check pressure in the cool of the morning. Never let air out of a hot tire. The proper level of air in your tires is all there is between you and the road surface. This is a good place to suggest a tire pressure monitoring system. It works all the time and can also monitor tire temperature. It will warn when any tire falls below a preset pressure or temperature so you can stop before you have a blow-out. There are many different systems on the market. I suggest you consider a system with replaceable sensor batteries. This is so you won't have to buy new ones when the batteries die.

There are many other things that must be checked to keep your rig ready to go, and every rig is different. What I have listed above is a minimal list, and you must look for those other things. There are many resources available to help you with maintenance and repair of RV systems and appliances. I have the Trailer Life RV Repair and Maintenance Manual by Bob Livingston. It is available at Camping World and other RV supply stores. There are also numerous video's available for purchase on the internet to help with rig maintenance.

Chapter 23 What About Holding Tanks?

Almost all RVs today have holding tanks for water and waste. These and extra batteries make modern RVs "self-contained". There are usually three main storage tanks in a camper or motor home. They are the Fresh Water, Gray Water, and the Black Water tanks. These holding tanks are great conveniences, but you must be knowledgeable, as well as understand the basic preventive maintenance that must be done to keep them working as designed.

Fresh Water Tank

The largest of the three types of holding tanks is the fresh water tank. These are mostly made of a plastic material. They can be either black or white. The black color will inhibit the growth of algae. We find that the larger the rig, the bigger the holding tank. Small rigs might have as little as ten to twenty gallon capacity. We have a ninety gallon tank, and I have seen some rigs with as much as a hundred and fifty gallon storage.

I think the quality of the water in the fresh water tank is a very important item. I mentioned algae earlier, and it and other bacteria can grow quite well in your tank if you don't pay attention to a few precautions. If you are a part time RVer, you should sanitize the fresh water tank before every trip, and full timers should do this yearly. It is a simple but lengthy process:

Sanitization of the Fresh Water tank

Start with a nearly full fresh water tank.

Turn off the external water supply and turn on the water pump.

Turn the water heater off, and let the water cool.

Dilute 1/4 cup of household bleach for each 15 gallons of tank capacity in to a gallon of water. Don't pour straight bleach into your tank.

Add the chlorine/water solution to the water tank.

One faucet at a time, let the chlorinated water run through them for one or two minutes. You should be able to smell the chlorine

Top off the RV fresh water tank and let stand for at least three hours.

Drain the system by flushing all the faucets and the shower for several minutes each. Don't forget the outside shower if your rig is equipped with one.

Open the fresh water tank drain valve to speed up emptying the tank and open the hot water tank drain plug and drain until it is empty.

Close all valves and faucets and drain plugs.

Fill water tank with fresh water.

Turn off cold water supply.

Open a faucet in the RV to relive pressure.

Pull out handle of the Pressure Relief Valve and allow water to flow from the valve until it stops.

Release the handle on the valve. It should snap shut.

Close the faucet and turn on cold water supply. As the hot water tank fills, the air pocket will be replenished.

Flush each faucet for several minutes each repeating until the tank is again empty. Make sure you are using the water pump and not an external water supply.

Fill the tank again. The water should now be safe to drink but if the chlorine odor is too strong you can repeat the fresh water flush.

Your RV fresh water system should now be safe for use.

Water weighs about eight pounds per gallon. This means we are hauling seven hundred and twenty pounds of excess weight if we travel with a full tank. Fear not, we don't do it. We put about a quarter of a tank in when we travel so we can flush the toilet with a little left for hand washing. I try to dump the fresh tank as often as possible to maintain fresh and clean water. Most campgrounds will let you do this on your campsite.

We discussed water filters and water pressure regulators in the "What other stuff will you need?" chapter. Please understand that water quality varies from place to place, and you must filter the water you put in your rig. Water pressure also varies from campground to campground. Some have in excess of one hundred pounds per square inch pressure. Modern rigs are designed for less than fifty. If you do not use a water pressure regulator, you could rupture an interior water hose. Believe me; you do not want to clean up after that, not to mention the expense of a very difficult repair.

Winterization

If you aren't a full-timer yet, you will probably need to winterize your fresh water system. Winterizing can be a simple process, if you just follow the steps below. There are other ways to do this; I have given you the most common.

If your rig does not have one, an important accessory you can add to your RV is a water heater by-pass. It is a simple device; one or two valves that isolate the tank from the rest of the water system. A water heater tank is normally about 7 gallons. If you do not have one of these, you will have to fill the tank with seven more gallons of expensive RV antifreeze than you need. Installation is a pretty simple do it yourself project, or any RV dealer can install it for you. You will save the cost of the valve in just a few years with the value of the antifreeze you save.

RV antifreeze is safe to use in drinking water systems. Please do not use automotive antifreeze as it is poisonous and can cause serious illness and possibly death.

So let's get started. Here are the steps for winterization:

Drain fresh water tank.

Drain hot water heater.

Dump and flush both black and gray water holding tanks, leave gray water valve open.

Turn off fresh water supply

Screw a compressed air adaptor into the fresh water inlet. The adapter is available from Camping World or most RV dealers.

Apply compressed air, keeping the pressure less than twenty pounds per square inch.

Open each faucet, one valve at a time, allowing the compressed air to force the water out of the line. Don't forget the shower and toilet.

Remove the drain plug from the hot water tank and allow the compressed air to blow out the remaining water. Reinstall drain plug.

Disconnect the compressed air and the adapter.

Close the water heater by-pass valve.

Remove the water line that runs between the fresh water pump and the fresh water tank, where it joins the fresh water tank. There is an inexpensive adapter kit to make this easy and it is available from most RV parts dealers.

Insert the end of the line into a gallon jug of RV antifreeze. (Again, do NOT use automotive antifreeze.)

Start the fresh water pump. It will run for a few moments, sucking antifreeze from the jug. It will stop as pressure in the system builds up.

Open each valve of each faucet, one at a time, until the red antifreeze appears; then shut the faucet. Don't forget the shower, toilet, and outside shower.

Remove the line from the jug of antifreeze and reattach it to the inlet side of the water pump or close the valve if you have an adapter.

Pour a cup or two of antifreeze into each drain including the shower.

You're done!

Grey Water Tank

The grey tank is designed to collect and store the water that goes down the sink and shower drains and from a clothes washer if you have one. This water has soap and detergent in it but no sewage so it is called Grey Water. The tank is designed with a capacity that varies with the size of the rig. You should have enough capacity to hold up to a week's worth of grey water from two people. This probably does not include use of a washing machine. The grey water tank is the biggest constraint to boon docking, or living off the grid without external utilities. It is usually almost equal or slightly larger than the black or sewer tank.

Campgrounds do not allow the dumping of Grey Water onto the ground at a site. It must be dumped at the same Dump Stations as the Black Water tank.

To this end, the standard for grey water and black water tank dumping connections is the same for all campers and RVs.

When you look in the service compartment of an RV, or under a camper, you will recognize the same 3-inch connectors; and on most RVs, the black water and grey water lines go to a T-type connection with one common 3-inch connector. This is for ease of connecting and dumping of waste.

Black Water Tank

The black water tank holds the water that goes down the toilet. Some rigs with two toilets may have two black tanks. I can't imagine why, but there are some instances of a manufacturer building a rig with only one holding tank that contains the grey water and the black water. I'm sure this saves some money, but I don't think the designer ever traveled and camped in an RV.

It is easier to clean out a sewer hose with soapy grey water than any other way. That's why it is recommended that you dump the black water first, then the grey. Doing this will allow the grey water to flush out the waste that is left in the hoses from the dumping of the black water tank, and helps clean the hose system, leaving only (or at least mostly) Gray Water waste in the hoses.

In the chapter where I covered buying sewer hose, I recommended you have plenty to reach distant sewer fittings. This did not mean hooking all of them up and letting them flop around on the ground in a heap of coils that look like a resting boa constrictor. Use only as much as you need to make a straight run and elevate it off the ground with one of the many available types of plastic gadgets made for that purpose.

When you check into a campground, you will be given material about the rules; often there will be a statement telling you to use a threaded sewer connector. Other instructions may tell you to use a rubber sewer gasket to seal up the space between your sewer hose and the campground sewer connection. Please read these instructions and heed them as local ordinances direct these actions.

Toilet Paper

Here is the scoop on toilet paper for use in an RV. Unless you like to throw money down the toilet, don't buy the expensive "RV" brand. Many other common brands work quite satisfactorily. What you need to know is that it will break down in the tank. To test toilet paper, place a few sheets in a covered cup of water. Gently shake it for a minute. Remove the top and the paper sheets should be shredded into pieces. If not, it probably will not break down in your tank either.

Toilet Chemicals

There are probably hundreds of chemical products to put in the black tank. Most are to cut down on odors. Others add chemicals to help break down and liquefy the waste. Whatever you use, try to stay away from any product using formaldehyde. This is definitely an environmentally unfriendly chemical and will kill the beneficial bacteria in septic systems. Try to find an enzyme based product. We use a tablet type, but it also comes as a powder, liquid, and even a premixed, dissolvable pack. Unfortunately, these enzymes will not work in very hot or very cold temperatures. We solved the hot weather issue with a product called "Odorcon" which contains stabilized chlorine dioxide. This stuff works great. Check them out at http://www.3rodorcon.com/ . They also have a great product for your fresh water tank.

Flushing the Toilet

When you step on that pedal, hold it down for a while. More water in the black tank will make it easier for the enzymes to work. Some toilets have another pedal position that will allow you to add water without flushing.

Dumping and Rinsing the Black and Grey Holding Tanks

OK, you have set up your sewer hose, tightened everything up and have two full tanks. Let the fun begin. Not so fast. It is a wise person who plans ahead. When the black water comes cascading down that three inch hose, there is a lot of weight behind it. When it is turned loose, it could lift that sewer hose right out of the connection if it isn't tightly threaded or weighted down with several pounds of weight on top of that end of the hose. We spared no expense on this device. I found the worst and most stretched out pair of sweat socks I could find, filled each with gravel, tied them together, and draped it over the business end of the sewer hose. It's hard to believe how much of that stuff will spread out on the ground and cover your shoes before you can close the valve. Whatever you want call it, this is nasty stuff. You may have heard this called the black water dance. Now you know why. The thing that an RVer learns very quickly is that this is **not** a septic tank, but just a temporary holding device for some extremely nasty stuff!

This tank was designed to hold the excrement, urine and toilet paper of a typical couple for about a week. Please do not put anything else down there. If you accidentally drop something you want to keep down there, rethink it. The complications and downright nastiness of a clogged black tank are not worth it.

Hopefully you purchased a short clear section of plastic sewer pipe attached just below the dump valve. This will allow you to see when the dump is complete and see the condition of the flush water. Did I mention that you should wait until the tank is nearly full before you dump? Here we go. First you will want to pull the black tank valve handle all the way out. You will be rewarded by a rush of brown stuff followed by a gurgle. Hopefully, your rig is equipped with a built-in black tank rinse system. This is one or two nozzles plumbed into the side of the black tank to rinse out the interior. Hook a short water hose up to the rinse hose connection and start the water running. You will see all kinds of stuff flowing out of the tank you just dumped. Keep this up for a minute or so and then close the black tank valve while the water is running. This will start to fill the black tank with water. At this critical point, do not let yourself become distracted. This is because the black tank has a vent to let sewer gasses escape out of a fitting on your roof. If you forget to turn off the water, the tank will fill and there will be strange noises coming from the toilet. Do not step on the flush valve unless you want to be rewarded with an explosive shower. In short order, the water will start to rise through the vent pipe and provide you with a really good reason to clean your roof. Wait no more than about eight minutes for a forty-five gallon black tank and pull the black tank valve. The extra water will do a good job of removing stuck toilet paper from the sides of the tank. At some point, the clear section should show the water running clear. At that point, the tank is clean and rinsed. Let several gallons of water run into the tank to coat the bottom with several inches of water. Close the black tank valve and open the grey tank valve. The grey water will run out as a solid stream and then finish with a rush of bubbles. A nearly full grey tank will do a good job of cleaning out the sewer hose. Now is the time to put the chemicals in the black tank.

Tank Sensors

Until quite recently, the sensors inside the holding tanks were metal rods threaded through the side of the tank at intervals to indicate the liquid level in the tank. This works quite well in fresh and grey water tanks. Unfortunately, toilet paper remnants and other stuff will get hung up on these and the tank monitor will usually read much higher than what it really is. The only sure cure I know of is to have the tank professionally steam cleaned. The folks who do this have a video camera attached to the hose and they can find and remove all the remaining stuff in the tank. This costs around four hundred dollars for both the black and grey yanks and is the only way I know of to get those pesky sensors clean. Guess what? It won't be long and they will be clogged again. Newer sensors are taped to the outside surface of the tank and are quite accurate. Retrofit kits are available that use existing wiring.

At a Campsite

When you pull in to a campsite, one of the first things you will do is hook up your sewage connector to the one at your site. Even though you hook up, DO NOT open any valves until the tanks are full. If you dump a partially filled black tank, there won't be enough volume to remove most of the waste. There was a time when we left our grey valve open all the time, but now we keep it closed until it is full. Typically we dump grey twice as often as black. We will do it more often when using the washing machine. Please do not leave the black tank valve open all the time. The waste will harden due to a lack of water in the tank, and you will soon find out what we mean by pyramiding. You will eventually clog up the black tank and will have a very expensive tank pressure cleaning job to look forward to. Leave the valve closed, and open only when full and ready to be dumped.

On the Road

Some folks will leave a site and drive to the next campground in the same day. They will dump the black water tank and fill it with water for the trip. This will allow the water to shake around during the bumps and turns of the trip, and can then be dumped again when you arrive at the next site. This agitation during the trip can really help clean the tank. We have heard that putting ice cubes down the toilet will help this agitation. Unfortunately, the ice will melt quickly. Another idea is to put about ten pounds of rock salt of the type used in ice cream freezers into the black tank. This should last longer than the ice.

Chapter 24 Our Favorite Essential Gadgets

In this chapter, I have picked out what I feel are some of the most important items we have purchased for our rig. Most are applicable to any type of RV be it motorized or towable.

Surge Guard 50A Surge Suppressor

We bought the Surge Guard 50A Hardwire - Model 34560 Rated 120/240V, 50A. We got it less than a week after we picked up our rig. This will protect all the sensitive electronics in your rig from surges and brown-outs. There is a thirty amp model available, as well. This can be installed by someone who understands electrical wiring. We bought it at Camping World, but you can check out the company's offerings at http://www. http://www.trci.net/ What follows is from the manufacturer's data sheet.

This 50 amp Surge Guard product monitors shore power continuously and shuts off when it detects excessive voltage or open neutral conditions that could damage electronic equipment in your coach. Like its thirty amp partner, the 50 amp hardwire unit is permanently installed within the bay of your coach, preventing potential theft and damage from the elements. Some additional features include:

The unit provides automatic reset on power restoration.

Automatically shuts off the power when the following is present: Open neutral, Low (<102V) and High (>132V) Voltage

Caution indicator light indicates: Miswired pedestal, Reverse polarity, Elevated ground voltage

2 minute 15 second reset delay protects A/C compressor.

1750 Joules of power surge protection.

Battery Watering System

The first time I tried to check the water level in the battery, I almost had to remove all the large gauge wiring from the battery tops to open the cell covers. Then it was hard to see the level in the cells to the back of the battery compartment. Enter the Pro-Fill RV battery watering system. We bought this from Camping World, but it should be available elsewhere. Check it out at http://www.flow-rite.com/ . Here is some material from the manufacturer:

Pro-Fill On-Board Battery Watering System, 6-volt RV Edition, provides the most convenient and accurate means of filling and maintaining proper battery water levels. Hard to reach batteries are just as easy to fill as batteries on a workbench. Several batteries can be filled safely and simultaneously from a single remote position without ever having to touch a battery or remove a cap. Pro-Fill's automatic control valves ensure each cell is closed when the precise level is reached.

Fill up to six batteries in seconds from a single fill point

Fits all standard 6V lead acid batteries

Eliminates need to remove vent covers to fill

Automatically sends water to low cells only

Installs in minutes, no tools required

Safer and more accurate than conventional filling

Improves battery life and performance

Hard to reach batteries are as simple to fill as batteries on a workbench

Several batteries can be connected and filled at the same time

Automatic shut-off prevents over or under watering

Simple hand pump operation

Use with any distilled water container

Quick disconnect feature allows supply to be attached in a snap

No need to remove vent covers

Three stage Water Filter

During our homework period before we bought our rig, I learned a lot about water quality and different methods of filtration. The best information I got was from The RV Water Filter Store at http://www.rvwaterfilterstore.com/ . These guys know their stuff. They have a store during the winter months at the Yuma, AZ, flea market. You can also order online. I decided to build a three stage filter that could later be upgraded to a reverse osmosis unit. I bought three Culligan brand canisters at a hardware store along with all the brass fittings needed to complete the project. The first has a twenty micron sediment filter; the second has a one micron sediment filter; and the third has a carbon block filter inside the canister. A painter steel top from the RV Water Filter Store completed the project. I've been using this setup for eight years with no problems. Just change the sediment filters when they get discolored and the carbon filter quarterly.

Tire Pressure Monitoring System
I had been reading about tire pressure monitoring systems for several years but I didn't buy one because of the non-replaceable batteries. Finally I found Truck System Technologies at http://www.tsttruck.com/ . They have an affordable system with user replaceable batteries. We bought the 507 system with ten sensors. Installation was fast and now we have peace of mind about all our tires. They have an updated system now with flow through sensors so you can add air with the sensors installed.

Aquajet RV Water Pump
We had not lived in our rig for more than a couple of months before we decided the original twelve volt water pump was inadequate. Mainly it didn't pump enough water at a high enough pressure. It was also noisy and irritating, and it would cycle during low flow conditions. It was hard enough to try to take a shower with it, but run the sink at the same time and forget about it. The Aquajet RV was a direct replacement for our old pump and produced 5.3 gallons per minute (gpm) at sixty five pounds per square inch (psi) of pressure. This is sufficient to give full flow with several fixtures in operation. We added a pair of two foot hoses to quiet down the operation and it hasn't given us any trouble for the five years we have had it. It was a little expensive; they are now about a hundred and seventy dollars at the RV Water Filter Store http://www.rvwaterfilterstore.com/ .

Water Pressure Regulator
Excessive pressure can cause your plumbing to leak or even rupture. It doesn't take long at high pressures to cause damage; even a fairly brief "spike" can do it. Pressure regulators are installed in your water supply line to limit the water pressure going into your RV. RV plumbing is normally rated around one hundred pounds per square inch, but you certainly don't need to use that much. Fifty to sixty five pounds per square inch is a very

comfortable pressure for faucets and showers. Parks don't always have that much, but when they do, having a regulator designed for good flow and pressure adjustability will allow you to take advantage of that better pressure without creating a problem with standard RV plumbing systems. I built my first one from a household regulator and some brass fittings. I still have it, but it is heavy. I purchased a Valterra model A01-1117VP from Camping World several years ago and it's great. It is lightweight and compact. I have had to replace the pressure gauge. Other than that, it has been trouble free. The problem with these is that you have to remember to disconnect it and take it with you. I paid to have the old heavy one shipped to our next campground.
http://www.campingworld.com/shopping/item/adjustable-water-regulator-lead-free/49511

Rhino-Flex Sewer Hose

I have used several brands of sewer hose through the years, but none are as good as the Rhino Flex model from Camco. It has among the thickest outer coverings in the industry and the only leaks I have had were caused by me. Don't use a weed eater anywhere near your sewer hose. Trust me on this one. I bought mine from WalMart for a little over $25 and I added a ten foot extension hose to reach out to twenty five feet. There is a new model of the Rhino Flex out now that is crush proof, but I haven't tried it. I also have two older ten foot sewer hoses from another manufacturer that I use when I need the extra distance.

Homemade Jack Pads

I described these in the chapter on setting up a campsite. I bought a fourteen foot two inch by twelve inch pressure treated board and had it cut at the lumber yard. It was cut into twelve one foot lengths. I laid two pieces with the grain running at right angles to one another. Then I screwed them together with three inch galvanized deck screws. Next I attached some heavy duty chrome one inch screw eyes to one side so I could reach the pad with an awning rod. I store the six of them in two plastic milk crates in a basement bay. I usually use these as jack pads, but they can be driven on if I need them to help level the rig. That's why I made six of them. Normally we use two packages of plastic jack pads to drive on.

Telescoping Cleaning Handle

I was at a rally and found the Mr. Long Arm Model 7508. This stores at four feet and extends to seven. It has a threaded end that fits most brushes and squeegees. I can easily reach the top of the sides of our rig and it makes windshield cleaning a breeze. It's quite sturdy and almost two inches thick. It doesn't bend when extended. Check it out at http://www.mrlongarm.com/ . They are found at most larger hardware stores.

Two Pound Sledge

We picked this up at a hardware store in Quartzite, AZ a few years ago. This is a hand-held sledge hammer that's great for hammering in ground stakes for anchoring patio mats as well as pounding in the center post for our flag pole. I've used it many times around the rig. This was a great buy for around ten bucks. Sorry, no website here, but I'm sure you will find one at a hardware store.

Gerber Multi-Tool

I carry this everywhere and use it several times every day for cutting, gripping, and opening things. There's no model number on it, but it is made of stainless steel and has seven tools besides the main blade and the pliers. I think I've had it for almost twenty years. It has kept me from having to open the toolbox many times.

Oxygenics Showerhead

I have no idea how we lived without this marvelous showerhead. We have probably bought three or four others and they all had the same problem. When there was low camp water pressure, it was almost impossible to have a good shower. When we got this one, we couldn't believe the difference. Depending on park pressure, we had to turn it down a few times. We got the chrome model at Camping World, but they can be found on Amazon.com cheaper. It comes in white, chrome, and brushed nickel. Be sure to get the wand holder too. It is made for the Oxygenics and will hold it at a great angle. Here are a few benefits from the company literature:

Maintenance Free - The Body Spa will never require maintenance or upkeep, making it completely easy to care for.
Limited Lifetime Warranty - Showerheads are guaranteed for life never to clog because the internal components are constructed using Delrin, which prevents mineral deposits, lime, and scale buildup.

Easy to Install and Operate - the Body Spa installs in seconds, comes with easy to understand instructions, and is a snap to operate. Everything you need is included so there is nothing else to buy.

Cost Effective - Because our showerheads last forever, require no maintenance, and are designed to conserve 30-70% of water and energy used by traditional showerheads, there is no better option for the RV owner that wants a cost effective solution. The affordable price helps too!

Self- Pressurizing - The patented technology uses a self-pressurizing design to increase spray velocity to produce a sensational experience even with low water pressure. This gives the user an invigorating clean-rinsing shower - anytime, anyplace.

Gets the Job Done - Water is energized and texturized with oxygen, speeding up the flow of the water and allowing for a clean rinsing shower. Shampoo and soap are thoroughly and quickly rinsed out.

Customize the Flow - The Body Spa works so well, that some people actually need to turn it down! The flow control valve lets the user customize their shower from 'soft and relaxing' to 'pulsating and massaging.' No matter what, the user will get a pleasant full coverage spray.

Health Benefits - the Oxygenics technology increases oxygen content in the water by up to 10 times! The oxygen helps to purify the water by creating negatively charged ions that counter damaging free radicals. The result is rejuvenated, younger looking skin.

Wilson SOHO AG55 Cellular Amplifier and Antennas

No matter what cellular carrier you use, there will be times when you are in a fringe area or even a no signal area. There is no help for the latter. If there is no tower in range, there will not be a signal no matter what you do. In the fringe areas and where there are obstacles to the signal such as hills and buildings. Since we started doing our weekly podcast, we absolutely must have good cellular reception in order to transmit our show file to the internet. I have had a Wilson Trucker antenna for several years that will connect to our Verizon air card. This has been helpful in many places, but not all. We recently purchased a Wilson SOHO AG55 wireless cellular amplifier and a directional inside antenna. Now I mount the Trucker antenna on a PVC mast and secure it to the ladder in the rear of the coach. I run coaxial cable to the amplifier in the cockpit.

It is in turn connected to the receiving antenna hanging from an interior compartment door. The Verizon air card is placed in close range to the inside antenna. Now we have amplified signals wirelessly transmitted inside the coach. This works with our cell phones as well as the Air Card. Now I get a four bar signal on the air card where there was no signal before. This was about $350 package I put together on Amazon.com. I highly recommend this and other Wilson products. Check out http://www.wilsonelectronics.com/ for a selection of what is available and then go to Amazon.com for the best prices. Another good source for this type of equipment is the Three G store at http://3gstore.com/ .

MBR-95 Wireless Router

I have used a wireless router from the Cradlepoint Company for several years. When I had an earlier three G air card, we had a Cradlepoint wireless router hooked up to it to provide a wireless "cloud" inside the rig so we could connect two computers and a wireless printer. When we got the new four G air card, we had to update to a router that could support four G air cards. Enter the MBR 95. To quote from company literature, "The MBR95 Wireless N Home Router provides a simple and secure way to add high-speed networking to the home. Designed specifically for multimedia, gaming and home computers, the MBR95 shares a Cable, DSL or 3G/4G Internet connection throughout the home wirelessly at 802.11 N speeds or through any of the four Ethernet ports."

"Supported devices include PCs, laptops, Macs, iPad, DVRs, gaming systems, cameras, printers and VoIP phones. To provide a safe networking environment, the MBR95 provides a wide variety of security features to prevent unwanted access, and robust content filtering to prevent children from accessing undesirable web content."

Now we have a cellular cloud and an internet cloud. For us, the primary gain with this device was to have a secure, hardware firewall so we can do banking securely. The MBR 95 is available from the three G store at http://3gstore.com/ . It costs $99 and comes with a one year technical service agreement with the three G Store technicians.

Jensen RV Hardened Television

When we had the interior of our rig remodeled a few years ago, they replaced the large, heavy, head knocker TV mounted above the cockpit with a Jensen thirty two inch HDTV. Jensen's televisions are hardened for RV use with rubber interior supports to withstand road vibration and shock. The cabinet and wall mount supports are reinforced as well. We have been quite happy with this TV and the price has come down some lately. This TV is available online and at Camping World.

Heavy Duty Satellite Antenna Tripod

We purchased a tripod from the TV4RV Company. Their heavy duty model was designed to handle large HD dish antennas in up to fifty mile per hour winds. The legs are adjustable and there is a built in bubble level to make set-up easy. Once leveled, a compass fits in the top to orient the tripod. Then put the dish on and you will be plus or minus two degrees from the optimum signal point. Dish setup and aiming has been reduced to less than five minutes. Check them out at: http://www.tv4rv.com/

Grill Pan

Sometimes it is just too hot, or it's raining, or it's too cold outside to fire up the grill to make dinner. We solved this with the grill pan. It looks like a shallow pan with ribs in the center. Ours is non-stick and is twelve inches across, so we can cook two steaks or four burgers at one time. It leaves nice grill marks on the meat too.

Wave 6 Catalytic Heater

We bought this heater at Camping World six years ago with boon docking in mind. It turns out we use it almost exclusively instead of our gas furnaces. The unit uses no electricity and is super-efficient on gas usage. We put in a tee from the range top and ran a gas line down to the floor by the refrigerator with a quick disconnect fitting. There is a twelve foot gas hose attached to the Wave 6 so we can position it anywhere to get good coverage. This six thousand BTU heater has kept us warm every winter since we bought it. Check it out on Amazon at http://www.amazon.com/Camco-57341-Olympian-Wave-6-Catalytic/dp/B000BV01CK .

Logs and Records

We keep a record of all the campgrounds we stay in. When we started out on the road, we bought a book called Camper's Daily Log from Camping World. Later on we received a larger log from an Escapees friend. You could make one up for yourselves with whatever information that you want. Our new log has a page for each visit, the date, weather, where you traveled from, where you went to, and what roads did you travel (this is really good for secondary roads to help remember the good, the bad, and the just plain ugly). Starting mileage and time and ending mileage and time is also included so we can keep track of the fuel expenses to include where we bought the fuel, the cost per gallon, how much we got, and of course the MPG. There is also a section on the page for what campground we stayed in and what services it had such as water, electric, sewer, cable, Wi-Fi, and nightly cost. We also rate the campground for cleanliness and friendliness, and comment on any interesting or special things about the campground. We write what we did there and any interesting places we visited like museums, parks, and food places. If we can, we keep the brochures and file them in another binder. In this one we have a sheet protector for each of the campground maps of the places we liked. We also put in restaurant menus and brochures from local area attractions that we might want to come back to and visit again. Many times this has been a great help, because we always find reasons to go back to an area and revisit. This way, we already know the campground with the best sites circled, and the best restaurants and attractions to go to. After many years of being on the road its fun to go back and remember the places we have seen and when we were there.

Many of you have seen the United States maps on the side of rigs and some or all of the states are filled in to signify that the owner of the rig has visited that state. Kathy has a rule that if we have stayed in the state and have at least spent one night, then the state gets to be filled in on the map. We put our map on the inside of the door to be a conversation starter when we are sitting outside. This is just the way we do it and you may decide to do it a different way. It's really is up to you what works best for your RVing lifestyle.

Photos and Blogs

We take loads of pictures when we travel to new places. Thank God for the digital camera. We try to get a shot of the sign announcing an attraction like a National Park or Monument. That way, we can easily identify the location of the following photos. Five years ago, we discovered a wonderful **free** software program from Google called Picassa. Google's Picasa software lets you organize, edit, and upload your photos in quick, easy steps. You can download Picasa at http://picasa.google.com. When you open Picasa, it simply looks at the folders on your computer and displays the photos it finds. It displays the file types that you tell it to find, in the folders that you tell it to search. When using editing tools in Picasa, your original files are never touched. The photo edits you make are only viewable in Picasa until you decide to save your changes. Even then, Picasa creates a new version of the photo with your edits applied, leaving the original file totally preserved. There are numerous share buttons in Picassa that let you upload your selected pictures to web albums, email, blogs, and others. We learned even more about this great software from our friends Jim and Christine Guld, also known as the Geeks on Tour. They teach classes on Picassa at rallies and computer clubs. Check them out at http://geeksontour.tv/ .

The folks at Geeks on Tour also got us started in blogging. The word blog is a contraction for web log. A blog gives you a place on the internet to record your travels in words and pictures to share with family and friends. They introduced us to a **free** program from Google called Blogger. Within five minutes, we had a blog up and running with one post up on the web. Check out Blogger at http://www.blogger.com/ . There are many thousands of blogs on the internet covering almost everything you can imagine. We follow ten or more blogs every day from other RVers.

Podcasts

We never knew what a Podcast was until we started producing one. According to Wikipedia, "A **podcast** is a type of digital media consisting of an episodic series of audio files subscribed to and downloaded through wed syndication or streamed online to a computer or mobile device." In 2008, we were wintering in Florida. Our oldest son was a radio producer and suggested we should do an RV radio show on Saturday mornings. We did that for four months until it was time for us to move on. The show was called

"Living the RV Dream". We enjoyed it and had already gathered a sizeable audience both locally and on the internet feed from the station. By then I had learned about podcasts and we decided to continue to produce Living the RV Dream on the road. We built a website to feature it as well as a place to put photos. Fast forward to 2012; one hundred and seventy weekly episodes and we are still having a ball doing the show. Check it out at http://www.livingthervdream.com .

We are now promoting podcasting as an audio version of a blog. The software to do the recording is free and so are some of the websites that distribute the files. Here are several other RV podcasts you might like: http://rvnavigator.com/ , http://newradio.com/RVDREAMRADIO/ , and http://www.thevap.com/ about vintage Airstream trailers.

Chapter 25 Lessons Learned

We learned most of these lessons personally; some were learned by other folks who passed on the wisdom to us. Most of these were those "Ah Ha" moments that we remember.

Awnings

I love our awnings. They give us shade and privacy, and occasionally grief. Automatic wind sensors that are supposed to retract your awning when the wind reaches about twenty five miles per hour do not always work.

It doesn't matter how many straps and hold downs you have, wind can destroy an untended awning very quickly.

The lesson learned here is to never, never leave your campsite without securing your large, expensive awning.

Always remember to check that the awnings are secure either when closed or open.
When leaving a campground in Oregon, our small awning over the left side of the rig was left out. The site was a little tight and the trees were close to the right side of the rig. So after putting the umbilical's away, John pulls out and I'm following in the car. I notice that the awning is out and I'm honking and yelling about the awning and people are pointing to it, but John just keeps rolling along. Fortunately he had to pull over to hook up the car and we were able to store it properly.
 We once saw a big rig pull out of a campground and the large, expensive, automatic awning on the passenger side was open. As he turned the corner it hit a light pole and the whole awning was ripped off of the RV. The sound was awful and, of course, everyone was looking. The expense of repair was in the thousands. Lesson learned. Do the walk around before traveling and double check just to be sure everything is put away and stored. This includes the crank-up TV antenna, as well.

Cellular Telephone Service

We have had a Verizon cell phone long before we started RVing. We were lucky because Verizon has had service almost everywhere we have been across the country. The other major cellular providers don't seem to have as good nationwide service. There are gaps, however, especially in sparsely populated areas in the west.

We have to put up a podcast file every week, and we need reliable phone service for our Verizon air card. Our solution was to add a Wilson wireless amplifier to boost weak signals. It works quite well, but the lesson learned is that you can't amplify a non-existent signal. You may have to drive to a town to get phone service.

Entry Steps

I don't seem to have trouble going out of the rig - it's the coming in. Twice now I have fallen into the rig, mainly because I have had too much stuff in my hands. The first time I really cut up my hand as I fell and hit the metal steps. The second time, I was on the last step and was wearing sandals, and the sandal caught on the step, and down I went, groceries and all. What a mess and not a pretty sight. Remember to have a light load into the rig. Lesson learned: don't take more than you can handle into the rig. Actually, always take a little less than you think you can handle.

Evacuation Plan

We have never had to evacuate because of a weather event or other natural disaster. Many RVers have, however. As I write this, fires are sweeping through Utah and are causing numerous evacuations. Severe weather seems to be the biggest problem we will normally face. We have gone through several hail storms in South Dakota where we moved to a bath house to avoid broken glass from the large hail stones. There are several lessons to be learned from severe weather. First, have a weather radio and have it on standby at all times. Find out what county you are in when you arrive at a campground. Program it and surrounding counties into a radio equipped with Specific Area Message Encoding. When threatening weather is approaching, go to a bathhouse or club house of block construction. Have a "Go" box with insurance information for your rig and car as well as a supply of required medications and a cell phone. Take the GO box with you. Find these substantial buildings as soon as you arrive at a campground, and plan how you will get to them. Do not stay in your rig during severe wind events. Straight line winds can tip even the heaviest motor home.

Fueling

After having to wash diesel fuel off my hands several times, I learned to have a pair of gloves specifically for fueling in an easy to reach place.

Although many commercial truck stops have RV islands, I don't use them anymore. They tend to be a tight fit and the pumps seem to run much slower than at the truck pumps. We have also had to wait while other less considerate RVers sit at the pump while they have lunch.

Holding Tanks

Oh, where do I start? I talked a little about "the black water dance" in an earlier section. When you buy a used rig, be very careful the first time you dump. Start with grey water for a short time to check for leaks around the valves. If there are some, don't try to pull the black valve unless you are ready to clean up the mess that will form in the bottom of your service bay.

Next and I repeat from earlier in the book, buy the sewer hose with the thickest side-walls you can find. Pinhole leaks tend to become larger as more "stuff" flows down the line. Also stay far away from any sewer hose with a weed-eater. It just isn't pretty when you don't realize how many little slices you just took into that thick walled hose.

The first accessory you should buy and place immediately after the valve assembly is a short, clear plastic section so you can see just what is flowing out of those tanks. You'll be really glad you did.

Have plenty of disposable rubber gloves as they tend to rip easily. You might even spring for a pair of heavy duty neoprene gloves. Just wash them thoroughly after you use them. For that matter, wash everything in your service bay remotely connected to dumping holding tanks at least every time you use it. This isn't funny; you can contract some very nasty infections from cross-contamination with fecal matter. Also, don't store your drinking water hose or water pressure regulator in the same compartment as your sewer hoses and accessories.

Get plastic caps for each end of every length of sewer hose you carry and use them. Even clean sewer hoses smell like, well, you know.

If your campground sewer connection is not the screw-in type, make sure you have adequate weight on the end of the hose that goes into the ground. If you don't, you may do everything right, and as soon as you pull that black tank valve, the business end of the hose will jump out of that hole like a cowboy being bucked off a horse. It's hard to describe how fast a flood of nasty, smelly, brown sludge will spread all over the ground before you can close the valve. Let me tell you, at that time, feeling helpless is the least of your problems. I filled two old sweat socks with gravel and tied them together. They do the trick, but I still keep a close eye on the ground fitting.

Here's a lesson someone else learned the hard way. When flushing your black tank with an installed tank flushing system, pay close attention to how long you leave the water turned on with the black valve closed. If you manage to fill the black tank and the toilet seal holds, the only outlet for all that pressurized sludge is up the vent pipe to the roof. I just don't even want to think about cleaning that mess up.

Disconnecting Fresh Water

You are all set to pack up and leave the campground and now it's time to disconnect and stow the fresh water hose. Not so fast young grasshopper. When you turn off the park fresh water supply either by a pump handle or a rotating spigot, there is still pressure in the RV water system. If it is a really hot day, you might enjoy a short, intense shower, but usually you want to stay dry and go drive your rig. I put a "Y" connector at the output side of the water pressure regulator to attach a water hose for washing or other use while in camp. Get out of the way and open the valve on the unused side and pressure will be relieved out of that port. Yes, this has happened to me, twice. It's really hard to laugh at yourself when you are soaking wet and mad to boot.

Once you roll all the water out of the hose and roll it up, connect the ends together to keep it clean. Next lesson learned is to remember to unscrew the water pressure regulator. It is quite expensive to ship these around the country. Be sure and store it with the hose in a compartment without sewer hoses.

Hooking up Your "Toad"

The lesson learned here is: practice, practice, practice. There are a number of steps that must be performed to successfully hook up a towed car to a motor home. Almost without fail, you, the new RVer will have to do this in front of an audience at the check-in. There will also likely be someone behind you waiting to check in.

They will be staring at you, too. Our recommendation is to find a church parking lot or an unoccupied large store lot and practice the unhooking and the hooking up. Do it enough times so you both can work together and get it done right every time. Avoid the embarrassing fumbling in front of the appreciative audience.

This lesson also applies to hooking up your rig once you have parked in your campsite. Practice enough so you know where everything is located, and develop a checklist for hooking up.

Whether unhooking or hooking up your toad, or setting up your campsite, there will often be well-meaning folks who either want to talk or to "help." Do not let this happen. You will become distracted and forget an important step in the process. Try to be tactful and explain you have a system and you will talk to them after you are finished. Imagine you are almost done hooking up and are about to put the weight on the end of your sewer hose when the next door neighbor comes over to talk. I don't have to tell you again the possible consequence of not having weight on the park connection.

Internet Service
Having connection to the internet is getting to be a "must have" these days. Many parks have Wi-Fi available, either free or for a fee. Some of these are fast and reliable while others barely creep along. The lesson to be learned here is that public Wi-Fi is not secure. Unscrupulous people with the right equipment can monitor everything you do on the internet. Because we do all our banking on the internet, we require a secure connection at all times. That is why we use a wireless router with our Verizon air card. It provides a hardware firewall with powerful encryption of our transmissions. A side benefit is that it provides a secure internet "cloud" within our rig so we can use other wireless devices like printers and other computers. We use a cellular amplifier to boost cell reception so we will have secure internet in fringe areas.

Kitchen
I seem to have most of my lessons learned at the kitchen. I like to make a protein shake, and I have a little top heavy stick blender. So, thinking I could leave it in the container and go get some more ice... let's just say the whole floor was mopped that day more than

once, and the dog was full of energy. Lesson learned: never think you are smarter than the law of gravity

I just love our smoke detector; it makes a wonderful noise, especially when I am cooking. They seem to place the smoke detector right above the stove, so any time I cook, that noisy thing goes off. Of course, I never remembered to unplug it when I cook, so every time I would cook something on the stove, the racket would start. John, the gadget man, comes in on his white horse to rescue me. He does research on the internet and finds a smoke detector that can be disabled by a push of the button for about 10 minutes. Lesson learned: there is always an answer to the problem - you just have to find it. It's usually on the internet.

Maps and GPS Lie

We were on an interstate highway looking for fuel. My GPS and the Next Exit indicated a stop coming up and I saw the sign for it just ahead. Unfortunately, at the end of a pretty narrow road we ran into a barrier with "Closed" and "Out of Business" signs on it. The weeds in the road said the place had been out of business for quite some time. Well, we unhooked the car and I was able to make a fifteen point turn to go back the way we had come. Several lessons here, but the main one is to not get yourself in a place you can't turn around.

We were camped in a Thousand Trails park in Hershey, PA, several years ago. We took a day trip in the car and it got dark and we weren't sure how to get back. Never fear, Gertrude, our trusty GPS was there to take us home. We spent two hours driving down farm roads and country lanes and around detours with Gertrude squawking "Recalculating" constantly. To her credit, we did get back to the campground by the most convoluted route imaginable. It turns out that there were several other ways we could have gone that would have taken about forty five minutes. We only found this out the next day in the light and with several local folks telling us. The lesson here is that our GPS routed us by the most direct "as the crow flies" method. The detours were an added special attraction. If you can set your GPS for shortest way, try that.

Parking Your Rig

Just as in hooking up your towed car, the lesson here is: practice, practice, practice. No matter whether you have a motor home or a trailer, you should practice backing into a campsite before you set out on your journey. The best way we have found is to find a large church parking lot or a closed WalMart or other large store with an empty lot. Buy some rubber traffic cones; you can use them later on to mark a campsite. Set up the cones to mark the boundaries of an imaginary campsite. Then practice backing into that without knocking over the cones. This is the time for you and your partner to set up the signals you will use later in a real campground. A lesson I learned from this was to stop and *not move* when you don't understand a signal. Eventually your honey will come to the window to investigate why you aren't moving. A Friday evening spectacle at many campgrounds is watching inexperienced folks try to park their rigs as the light is fading. The language can get a little rough, too. Another good lesson here is: if at all possible, plan to arrive at the campground at least two hours before sundown.

Propane System

The lesson here is to leave repair or maintenance on any propane appliance or other part of the propane system to an experienced RV service technician. They have the equipment and know-how to detect pressure drops and leaks. Remember, most RV fires are caused by propane problems, especially in refrigerators. If you have a twelve volt and propane refrigerator, check to see if it is covered in the major recall by the major refrigerator manufacturers. Ours was in the group. I took the rig in to an authorized service center to have the "fix" installed. Five months later, the unit stopped working. It turned out we had a leak in the refrigerant piping that could easily have led to a fire if we didn't have the fix in place. This was a huge lesson learned for us. Check the following sites for refrigerator recalls: http://www.norcoldrecall.com/ and http://www.dometic.com/enus/Americas/USA/RV-News/Dometic-Recall-Information/ .

Satellite TV

In our time on the road, we have used both Dish Network and Direct TV for our satellite TV service. The biggest difference I can see is that Dish will work in High Definition mode with dome antennas and Direct will not. Customer service for both can be wonderful one day and almost nonexistent the next. In any case, the main lesson learned here is that roof mounted antennas can easily be blocked by trees. It's relatively simple to carry an independent portable dish you can set up on a tripod and place wherever you have a clear shot at the southern sky. High Definition antennas can be large and heavy. You will need a heavy duty tripod for them.

Showers

Although our shower is small, it's comfortable. However, one thing to remember is to either leave the gray tank open, or make sure there is enough room left in the tank for the shower. So I'm in the shower, enjoying the wonderful feel of getting clean, when I notice that the water is up around my ankles: I think, "Oh boy, the drain is plugged." Well, in a very short amount of time, water was starting to over flow the shower stall and John is nowhere in sight or sound! I'm yelling his name - he is not answering me, I'm without clothes and water is going everywhere. Let's just say that I spent the rest of the afternoon cleaning the bathroom and not talking to John until I calmed down (it really wasn't his fault) and took another shower. Lesson learned: It is good to keep water in the grey tank to clean your sewer hose, but check the level in the grey tank (if the tank is closed) before taking a shower.

WalMart Stops or Wallydocking

There will be occasions where you may stop for the night in a WalMart parking lot. The lesson here is to immediately go inside to get permission to park overnight from a manager. Unless local ordinances prevent it, the manager will likely agree and even direct you to an area of the lot where you should park. If you ignore this advice, do not be surprised to get a knock on your door at 2:00 AM and find the local constabulary directing you to leave *immediately*.

Another lesson learned the hard way is to park with a clear lane to depart in the morning. You may be parked in what you think is a good spot and when you wake up, ten more rigs are parked all around you. Plan ahead.

This is a good place to talk about RVers' etiquette in parking lots as developed by the Escapees RV Club, and now endorsed by most other RV groups.

Industry-Sanctioned Code of Conduct

(RVers' Good Neighbor Policy)

1. Stay one night only!

2. Obtain permission from a qualified individual.

3. Obey posted regulations.

4. No awnings, chairs, or barbecue grills.

5. Do not use hydraulic jacks on soft surfaces (including asphalt).

6. Always leave an area cleaner than you found it.

7. Purchase gas, food, or supplies as a form of thank you, when feasible.

8. Be safe! Always be aware of your surroundings, and leave if you feel unsafe.

Water Leaks

If you detect water leaking into your rig, investigate immediately before the repair costs are out of sight. Water will run in the most direct path of gravity and this can be sideways. Our lesson learned was a leak in our slide-out roof that eventually caused the cabinets underneath to loosen and sag. If you can't find the leak source, have it checked out by a qualified RV service technician as soon as possible.

Weight and Overloading

Your rig and tow vehicle or towed car should be weighed when you purchase it and periodically after that. Weighing should be done on each end of each axel. You will want to know if you are overweight front to back as well as side to side. Shift cargo around as much as possible to even the load. If you exceed the Gross Vehicle Weight (GVW), you are looking at tire failure, front end suspension damage (on motor homes) and frame damage (on towables). All of these can cost thousands of dollars to repair. Pay attention, because if your insurance company weighs the rig after a claim, they can, and probably will, deny a claim on an overweight rig. Once you know the weight, you can consult your tire manufacturer's charts for correct tire pressure to support that weight. The lesson learned here is those manufacturer's specifications are important. If you pay attention, you might save your life or at least a lot of money.

Windshield Wipers

I really don't mind driving in the rain - I just slow down and take my time. It is important, however, to remove the windshield wiper covers before moving down the road and needing to turn them on. Traveling in the south, you can get some real frog stranglers of rain. So, here I am driving and enjoying the beautiful day and thinking nothing could go wrong. Don't ever think those thoughts; it started to pour, and when I turned on the wipers, this big mess appeared on the windshield. With every swish more and more gunk was left on the window. Trying to pull over in traffic was a nightmare, but we managed, and poor John had to run out in the pouring rain to remove the covers. Let's just say he was not happy... I thought he looked really cute all wet. Lesson learned: Double check to make sure everything is stowed for travel.

About the Authors

Kathy and I are really just plain folks like you, but we live in a 39 foot RV instead of a house. Maybe we lost our minds a bit; but we're happy we did. I am retired from the U.S. Navy as well as a retired manufacturing Quality Manager. Kathy has worked extensively in the medical administrative field. We had traveled worldwide due to my naval service as well as locations on both coasts of our beautiful country. We would see the big bus conversions and Winnebago RVs on the interstates and we both said, "one day that will be us". We started dreaming in earnest in 2003, a year before my job was outsourced. We went to shows and visited dealerships just to see if we could really do this. We could. We took the plunge two years later after we sold our house in Florida and bought "The Dream Machine", our 2004 Fleetwood Expedition diesel motor home. Since then we have travelled through the states we used to fly over and discovered a unique and awesomely beautiful land that pictures do not give justice to. We have been volunteers, workampers, podcasters, and now authors. I hope you enjoy our book; and if you see us on the road, honk and wave.

Visit our website at: http://www.livingthervdream.com .

Visit us on facebook at: https://www.facebook.com/jnkhuggins

Email us at: mailto:johnandkathy@livingthervdream.com

Appendix I RV Clubs

There are many good RV clubs for folks new to RVing, weekend warriors, full-timers and all in between. These clubs provide information, services, and rallies with activities, entertainment or door prizes. An RV club is just that: a club. A group of likeminded folks who get together to have fun doing what they love. You can meet some great folks that may become lifelong friends. The measure of an RV club is its members.

Clubs with a General Interest

These clubs provide a variety of information and services. Most have an annual fee. Most hold rallies, trips and other social events.

Escapees RV Club – http://www.escapees.com The Escapees RV Club was founded by full-time travelers and grew as a support network and eventually expanded to nineteen RV parks for its members. There are over fifty special interest groups; local, regional and a national rally; and even the CARE center, which is a place you can live in your rig but get assistance with everyday living.

Good Sam Club – https://www.goodsamclub.com/ is the largest RV club with over a million members, and over 2000 local chapters. Good Sam Club provides discounts on campgrounds, fuel, and RV products. They offer members-only rates on insurance and reliable emergency road service. There are national rallies, local rallies, or Samborees, group RV trips called Caraventures, and other trips offered.

FMCA - https://www.fmca.com/ Family Motor Coach Association (FMCA) is a large club for RVers with motorized RVs. They have discounts on campgrounds, fuel and RV products, mail forwarding, and much more. They hold large national rallies as well as local chapter events which are held throughout the year.

NAARVA – http://www.naarva.com/ National African American RV Association promotes the goals and ethnicity of African/American RVers.

SMART –http://www.smartRVing.net/ The Special Military Active & Retired Travel Club (SMART) brings military veterans (active, retired, & honorably discharged) together to share camaraderie, travel, RVing, and to support our veterans. They provide information for the military RV family, and support welfare programs while "Seeing the Country We Defend."

RVing Women –http://www.RVingwomen.org/ RVing Women is a national network whose members come from across the U.S. and Canada. Established by and for women who are interested in RVing, they have 16 Chapters across the country that offer camping, educational, and social events. They are a diverse group of women who enjoy many indoor and outdoor activities and hobbies.

Membership Camping Clubs

This type of club usually requires an upfront fee and then annual dues to use the various resorts in their systems. You should look closely at the resorts and their location to determine if the membership is a good value to you. Kathy and I belong to Passport America, RPI and Thousand Trails.

Adventure Outdoor Resorts - http://www.aorcamping.com/ AOR has three hundred and twenty resorts in the United States and Canada. They are a private membership RV network of affiliated resorts, and are dedicated to providing members with exceptional outdoor vacation experiences.

Coast to Coast - http://www.coastresorts.com/ The resorts that are in the Coast to Coast network are totally private "for members only". Coast to Coast is affiliated with the Affinity Group, parent company of the Good Sam Club. There are hundreds of resorts in C2C.

Colorado River Adventures - http://www.coloradoriveradventures.com/ CRA has eight parks located in the southwest. This is a membership club with annual dues.

Passport America - http://www.passportamerica.com/ Passport America is a club everyone should join. Annual dues of about $44 per year get you half off at over 1600 campgrounds.

Resort Parks International - http://www.resortparks.com/ RPI's network includes 200 private RV resorts, 400 public RV campgrounds, cabins and hundreds of condominiums worldwide.

Resorts of Distinction - http://www.resortsofdistinction.com/ ROD has about sixty resorts around the country. A prospective member must pay a fee to join one property and pay dues annually.

Thousand Trails/ELS - http://www.thousandtrails.com/ Thousand Trails has eighty-two resorts mostly owned by its parent company, Equity Lifestyle Properties, Inc. There are also over three hundred ELS parks that can be used with a discount. Membership in Thousand Trails gives the member access to RPI with payment of an annual fee and also access to Enjoy America, a half price program in hundreds of private and public parks.

Western Horizons - http://westernhorizonresorts.com/ Western Horizons has seventeen owned and affiliate resorts with most located in the west.

RV Brand Specific Clubs

Many RV brands have RV clubs dedicated to the owners of that particular brand. Most have rallies and other member get-togethers. Most have annual dues. Some of the larger rallies will have factory technicians available to fix small problems with your rig. Check on your manufacturer's web site for more information.

Appendix II Links to other Websites

Fuel Price Lookups
Pilot and Flying J Truck Stops www.pilotflyingj.com/fuel-prices

Loves fuel stops http://www.loves.com/

TA Travel Centers http://www.tatravelcenters.com/

Truckmaster Fuel Finder http://www.findfuelstops.com/ This free tool lists the **cheapest diesel fuel prices** at truck stops between any two points in the United States, or every truck stop in a 100 mile radius around a specified city. You can follow the link from the truck stop results to a page with the amenities, map, and other details for the truck stop.

Gas Buddy http://www.gasbuddy.com GasBuddy can help you find cheap gas prices in your city. In total, they have 243 websites to help you find low gasoline prices. This is also an application for Android phones.

MapQuest Gas prices http://gasprices.mapquest.com/ This one helps you find alternative fuels like biodiesel and E-85, as well as gasoline and diesel. It can also find propane.

Refurbish your RV
Focal Wood Products http://www.focalwood.com/ Located in Nappanee, IN, this is the place to have their Amish craftsmen build custom furnishings for your RV.

Dave and LJ's RV Interior Design http://www.daveandljs.com/ Custom RV Interior Cabinetry by Dave and LJ's RV Interior Design They have been creating custom cabinets and living spaces in RV, Coaches and Motorhomes for twenty years. Located in Woodland, WA

Bradd and Hall www.braddandhall.com/ is a family business that has been serving the RV furniture and boat furniture industries for over 25 years. Through this experience they have gained extensive knowledge of the complexities of RV furniture, yacht furniture, marine furniture and boat furniture configurations. They're goal is to work personally with you - whether you're remodeling your entire interior or just need one piece of RV or boat furniture. You must be completely satisfied with the end result or they'll refund all your money plus shipping both ways, Guaranteed. Located in Elkhart, IN

Bontrager's Surplus, Inc. http://bontragers.com/ Bontrager's deals in "surplus" materials, which could be overstocked, discontinued, close-out, or scratch and dent items. They buy merchandise by the truck load from the RV and Mobile Home manufacturers and major industry suppliers in and around Elkhart, Indiana, the RV capital of the world. Whether you are a do-it-yourself RVer or a dealer, they have what you need! Located in White Pigeon, MI

Mentions on Our Podcast
Living the RV Dream http://www.livingthervdream.com This is our website. From here you can listen to our weekly podcasts and link to our blog and our on-line store. We have lots of pictures of our travels as well.

The RV Bookstore http://rvbookstore.com/ This on-line store has the world's largest selection of books, DVDs, eBooks, and more about RVs and the RV lifestyle.

The RV Travel Newsletter http://www.rvtravel.com/ is a weekly RV newsletter, available by subscription that provides a wealth of free information.

Gypsy Journal http://gypsyjournalrv.com/ This is the website of our friends Nick and Terry Russell. Nick writes the Gypsy Journal, a tabloid style newspaper devoted to the RV lifestyle.

Geeks on Tour http://geeksontour.tv/ Our friends Chris and Jim Guld will teach you everything you need to know about computing on the road.

TechnoRv http://www.technorv.com/ TechnoRV focuses on improving the security, safety and enjoyment of your RV experience through innovative, well designed, high quality products.

Coach-Net http://nmc.com/services/rv.aspx towing, flat tire assistance, fluid delivery, jump-starts, lockout service, mobile mechanic, appointment assistance… No mileage or dollar amount limits- no out-of-pocket costs! We use Coach-Net and are very happy with their services.

Suncoast Designers http://www.suncoastdesigners.com/ specializes in the repair and replacement of all types of RV windows. They service motor homes, travel trailers, 5th wheels and any others you can think of. They can repair foggy double pane windows quickly.

Inverter Service Center http://www.inverterservicecenter.com/ This is the place near Nashville, TN where we had our inverter repaired. This is one of only three similar businesses in the country.

MCD Shades http://www.mcdinnovations.com/ MCD makes the popular American Duo line of interior RV day/night window shades

RV Quickshades http://www.rvquickshades.com/ Installs easily! Simply place the included suction cups on the inside of your windshield where you can comfortably reach. We have these and we love them.

RV Driving School http://www.rvschool.com/ Their mission is to put on seminars and provide private instruction to owners so they know how to operate their vehicle safely. **Mac the Fire Guy** http://macthefireguy.com/ For over 13 years Mac McCoy has taught fire safety education at RV shows and rallies all over the country.

US Military Campgrounds and RV Parks http://www.militarycampgrounds.us/ This is a great resource to find Military Famcamps with directions and ratings.

RV Travel Checklists http://www.campertrails.com/travel-checklist.html This is a great website with downloadable RV checklists.

Changin' Gears http://changingears.com/index.shtml This is a comprehensive site with valuable information for the beginning and experienced RVer.

Boondockers Welcome http://www.boondockerswelcome.com/ At Boondockers Welcome you can connect with other RVers who have a location for you to dry camp for the night; it might be in their driveway or a field on their farm. The view may be of amber waves of grain or of the McDonald's parking lot... but it will be a free place to park where you don't have to worry about idling truck engines, security, or that dreaded knock on the window at 2 am.

RV Manufactured Housing Hall of Fame

http://www.rvmhhalloffame.org/ The Recreation Vehicle and Manufactured Housing Industries started with a common thread. That thread was "affordable housing" Although the industries took divergent paths in our current products, our roots are still there and together we share a state-of-the-art museum, library and Hall of Fame celebrating our heritage. We invite you to join us in a fascinating trip through the history of these two industries.

RV Park Reviews http://rvparkreviews.com/ These are real reviews written by campers who have stayed at these parks. Our All Stays App takes us here for park reviews.

Casino Camper http://www.casinocamper.com/ This site reviews RV friendly casinos across the nation.

NADA RV Values http://www.casinocamper.com/ This is the gold standard for retail RV prices and is a big help in either buying or selling an RV.

RV Service Reviews http://rvservicereviews.com/ We have used this site several times to evaluate a particular service shop.

Handgun Laws US http://handgunlaw.us/ This site is a must if you travel with firearms or plan to do so.

Low Bridges

http://www.aitaonline.com/Info/Low%20Clearances.html If you plan to travel off the Interstates or major secondary roads, this site can save a lot of time planning a route around low clearance bridges and tunnels.

Corps Lakes Gateway http://corpslakes.usace.army.mil/visitors/ This government site has information on US Army Corps of Engineers sites throughout the US.

Best of the Road http://www.bestoftheroad.com/ A great resource for the beginner sponsored by Rand McNally.

Work for RVers and Campers http://www.work-for-rvers-and-campers.com/ this is a good site to look for jobs on the road.

Rigid Industries https://www.rigidindustries.com/ This is a great web site for LED fixtures for RVers

RV Daily Report http://rvdailyreport.com/ this is an RV industry web publication with lots of good information.

RV News http://www.rvnews.com/ this is also an RV industry web publication with lots of good information.

The RV Doctor http://www.rvdoctor.com Gary Bunzer has a massive amount of information on RV repair and maintenance

RV-Recalls http://www.rv-recalls.com lists the latest RV recalls every month

Appendix III Glossary of Towing Terms

Note: many of the definitions below are not standardized throughout the towing products industry. For the definition of those terms we have tried to choose the definition most generally in use.

Ball mount — the part of the hitch system that supports the hitch ball and connects it to the tow bar or trailer coupler. Adjustable ball mounts allow a hitch ball to be raised or lowered in order to level the towing system.

Base plate — see "mounting bracket."

Binding — when the tow bar is difficult to detach because of excessive pressure, the tow bar is said to be "bound."

Car-mounted — a tow bar designed to be mounted and stored on the towed vehicle.

Class 1 rated hitch — hitch receiver with a capacity of up to 2,000 pounds and 200 pounds tongue weight.

Class 2 rated hitches — hitch receiver with a capacity of up to 3,500 pounds and 300 to 350 pounds tongue weight.

Class 3 rated hitches — hitch receiver with a capacity of up to 6,000 pounds and 600 pounds tongue weight. It is sometimes used to refer to a hitch with a 2-inch receiver, regardless of the weight rating.

Class 4 rated hitches — hitch receiver with a capacity of up to 10,000 pounds and 1,000 pounds tongue weight. (Many times any hitch with a capacity greater than 6,000 pounds is referred to as a class 4.)

Class 5 rated hitches — hitch receiver with a capacity greater than 10,000 pounds and 1,000 to 1,200 pounds tongue weight.

Converter — a "3-to-2 converter" converts the electrical signals in a tow vehicle with separate (3-wire) brake and turn signals to tow vehicles with combined (2-wire) brake and turn signals. Conversely, a "2-to-3 converter" converts the electrical signals from combined to separate.

Coupler — the component that connects the tongue of a trailer or tow bar to the hitch ball.

Curb weight — the total weight of a vehicle and all necessary fluids (water, coolant and oil) and a full tank of gas, when not loaded with either passengers or cargo.

Diode — Diodes allow the towed vehicle's brake and turn signal lights to mimic the motor home's (which is required by law) without damaging the towed vehicle's electrical system. They allow current to flow in only one direction, thereby eliminating electrical feedback, which could damage the towed vehicle's wiring, fuses or other electrical components.

Dry weight (or "DW," a.k.a. "Unloaded Vehicle Weight") — this is the weight of the motor home (or towed vehicle) without adding fuel, water, propane, supplies and passengers.

Fishwire — a technique used to install many automotive aftermarket accessories. For example, if the available space is too small to position an attachment bolt by hand, a length of wire is threaded onto the bolt and the bolt is maneuvered ("fishwire") into position using the wire, which is then removed.

Gross Axle Weight Rating (or "GAWR") — is the maximum allowable weight that a single axle (front or rear) can support. GAWR applies to tow vehicle, trailer, and fifth-wheel and motor home axles. The GAWR is typically listed on a data plate near the front of the vehicle.

Gross Combined Vehicle Weight (or "GCVW") — the actual weight of a towing and towed vehicle, including all passengers and payload.

Gross Combined Weight Rating (or "GCWR") — the maximum allowable weight of the combination of the motor home and towed vehicle (or the tow vehicle and trailer or fifth wheel). It includes the weight of the vehicles, the cargo, passengers and a full load of fluids (fresh water, propane and fuel).

Gross Vehicle Weight Rating (or "GVWR") — how much weight a vehicle is designed to carry, set by the manufacturer. The GVWR is typically listed on a data plate near the driver's doorframe, and includes the net weight of the vehicle, plus the weight of passengers, fuel, cargo and any additional accessories.

Hitch (or "receiver hitch") — a device which attaches directly to a tow vehicle, providing the connection to the ball mount and trailer. Note: tow bars are sometimes incorrectly referred to as hitches.

Hitch adaptor — fits onto the receiver tube of a hitch and converts it from one size to another (from 1¼" to 2", or from 2" to 1¼"). A hitch adapter may reduce the weight capacity to the rating of the adapter.

Hitch ball — the ball-shaped attachment on the ball mount onto which a coupler is attached. The coupler mounts and locks on top of the hitch ball and encompasses the hitch ball.

Motor home-mounted — a tow bar designed to be mounted and stored on the motor home.

Mounting bracket (a.k.a. "bracket" or "base plate") — connects the towed vehicle to the tow bar. All mounting brackets are bolted on to the sub frame of the towed vehicle.

Proportional braking — a supplemental braking system which brakes at the same time and intensity as the motor home is said to be "proportional."

Quick-disconnects — the connection point between the tow bar and the tow bar mounting brackets. These components allow the tow bar to be quickly connected and disconnected. There is one quick-disconnect ("QD") for the driver's side and one for the passenger side. Quick-disconnects also allow for the mounting of accessories.

Quick links — used to attach the safety cables. They look like one link in a chain, and have a nut which can be threaded up or down to open or close the link.

Safety cables/safety chains — required by law, safety cables connect the towed vehicle to the towing vehicle. They are a secondary safety device to hold the vehicles together if the towing system separates for any reason. (Safety chains are commonly used with trailers or fifth wheels)

Stinger — the part of the tow bar that inserts into the motor home's receiver hitch. A hitch pin and clip secure the tow bar to the motor home.

Supplemental braking — an independent braking system that brakes the towed vehicle in tandem with the motor home.

Tongue weight — the downward force exerted on the hitch receiver by the towed vehicle, which is typically listed by the manufacturer. Tongue weight should be between 10 and 15 percent of the towed weight.

Appendix IV Glossary

120 AC/12 DC/LP-gas – refers to the power sources on which RV refrigerators operate; 120 AC is 120-volt alternating current (same as in houses); 12 DC is 12-volt direct current (same as in motor vehicles); LP-gas. Some RV refrigerators can operate on two of the three sources, others on all three.

Adjustable Ball Mount - An adjustable ball mount allows the ball to be raised, lowered and tilted in small increments to allow fine tuning of the spring bar setup and to compensate for tow vehicle "squat," which occurs after the trailer coupler is lowered onto the ball.

Airbag - In RV terms, a sort of shock absorber positioned at the forward and rear axles of a motor home.

Airstreaming - Using an Airstream travel trailer as RV of preference. Towing an Airstream travel trailer.

Anode Rod - An anode rod, when used in a water heater, attracts corrosion causing products in the water. These products attack the anode rod instead of the metal tank itself. The anode rod should be inspected yearly and changed when it is reduced to about 1/4 of its original size. The rods are used in steel water heater tanks - an aluminum tank has an inner layer of anode metal to accomplish the same thing. Anode rods should not be installed in an aluminum tank!

Arctic Pack - - Also spelled Arctic Pac and Arctic Pak, an optional kit to insulate RVs for winter camping.

Auxiliary battery - Extra battery to run 12-volt equipment.

Axle Ratio - The final drive gear ratio created by the relationship between the ring and pinion gears and the rotation of the driveshaft. In a 4.10:1 axle ratio, for example, the driveshaft will rotate 4.1 times for each rotation of the axle shaft (wheel).

Back-up monitor - Video camera mounted on rear of motor home to assist the driver visually with backing up the motor home, via a monitor mounted in the driver's compartment or in a central area of the cab where it can be viewed by the driver from the driver's seat. These monitors are usually left in the 'on' position to also assist the driver with the flow of traffic behind the motor home and in watching a "towed" vehicle.

Ball Mount - The part of the hitch system that supports the hitch ball and connects it to the trailer coupler. Ball mounts are available in load-carrying and weight-distributing configurations.

Basement Model - An RV that incorporates large storage areas underneath a raised chassis.

Black Water - Waste (sewage) from the toilet that is flushed into a black water holding tank, usually located beneath the main floor of the RV.

Blueboy/Blue-Boy - Term for portable waste holding tank, often this plastic tank comes in a bright shade of blue, hence the term.

Boondocking - Camping in an RV without benefit of electricity, fresh water, and sewer utilities.

Bowtie - Reference to Chevrolet because of the "bowtie" trademark.

Box - Reference to motor home's "living space" on a class A, built from the chassis up.

Brake Actuator - a device mounted under the dash of a towing vehicle to control the braking system of the trailer. Most brake actuators are based on a time delay, the more time the tow vehicle brakes are applied the "harder" the trailer brakes are applied.

Brake Controller - A control unit mounted inside the vehicle that allows electric trailer brakes to become activated in harmony with the braking of the tow vehicle. This device can be used to adjust trailer brake intensity, or to manually activate the trailer brakes.

Breakaway Switch – is a safety device that activates the trailer brakes in the event the trailer becomes accidentally disconnected from the hitch while traveling.

BTU - British thermal unit - A measurement of heat that is the quantity required to raise the temperature of one pound of water 1 degree F. RV air-conditioners and furnaces are BTU-rated.

Bubble - Loose term for defining a variety of conditions; such as when describing the level of RV sitting. (For example: my RV is 'off-level' a half bubble; referring to a 'bubble-leveler' tool). This can also be used to describe a delamination condition.

Bump Steer - A term used to describe a condition where the front axle feels to be rapidly bottoming out on the jounce bumpers and transferred back through the steering column and steering wheel. There can be several different causes to the problem with different cures for each condition. Sometimes a simple fix such as shocks or a steering stabilizer; sometimes more detailed corrections needed for correcting serious manufacturing oversights.

Bumper-Mount Hitch - This type of hitch is available in two configurations: A bracket with a ball mounted to the bumper or a ball is attached to the bumper (typically on pickup trucks). These hitches have very limited RV applications.

Bumper-Pull - Slang term regarding the hitch or towing method for a conventional travel trailer or popup; receiver and ball-mount type hitch.

Bunkhouse - An RV area containing bunk beds instead of regular beds.

Cabover - The part of a type C mini-motor home that overlaps the top of the vehicle's cab, and usually contains a sleeping or storage unit.

Camber - Wheel alignment - Camber is the number of degrees each wheel is off of vertical. Looking from the front, if the tops of wheels are farther apart than bottoms, it means "positive camber". As the load pushes the front end down, or the springs get weak, camber would go from positive to none to negative (bottoms of wheels farther apart than tops).

Camper Shell – is a removable unit to go over the bed of a pickup truck.

Campground -- Any kind of park that allows overnight stays in an outdoor sleeping area. It can be accessible only by foot, by hikers or backpackers, or can be a well developed RV Resort Park.

Caravan - A group of RVers traveling together with their various RVs. Large caravans often space RVs five minutes or so apart with CB radios used for communication between the various RVers. The end vehicle is sometimes called the "tailgunner" and it's the occupants watch out for a caravan member that may have had road trouble in order to assist, however possible.

Cassette Toilet - Toilet with a small holding tank that can be removed from outside the vehicle in order to empty it.

Castor - Wheel alignment - The steering wheels' desire to return to center after you turn a corner.

Chassis Battery - Battery in motor home for operating 12 volt components of drive train.

Class A Motor home - An RV with the living accommodations built on or as an integral part of a self-propelled motor vehicle. Models range from 24 to 40 feet long.

Class B Motor home –is also known as a camping van conversion. These RVs are built within the dimensions of a van, but with a raised roof to provide additional headroom. Basic living accommodations inside are ideal for short vacations or weekend trips. Models usually range from 16 to 21 feet.

Class C Motor home - An RV with the living accommodations built on a cutaway van chassis. A full-size bed in the cabover section allows for ample seating, galley and bathroom facilities in the coach. It is also called a "mini-motor home" or "mini." Lengths range from approximately 16 to 32 feet.

Coach - Another name for a motor home

Cockpit - The front of a motorized RV where the pilot (driver) and co-pilot (navigator) sit.

Condensation - Condensation is a result of warm moisture-laden air contacting the cold window glass. Keeping a roof vent open will help to reduce the humidity levels. Those added roof vents help to prevent cold air from dropping down through the vent while still allowing moist air to escape. Using the roof vent fan when showering or the stove vent fan when cooking also helps prevent excess moisture buildup.

Converter - An electrical device for converting 120-volt AC power into 12-volt DC power. Most RVs with electrical hookups will have a converter, since many of the lights and some other accessories run on 12-volt DC.

Covered Camper Wagons/Tepees – are canvas-covered wagons with or without electricity. Typically accommodates four or more people.

Coupler - The part of a trailer A-frame that attaches to the hitch ball.

Crosswise - A piece of furniture arranged across the RV from side to side rather than front to rear.

Curb Weight - The weight of a basic RV unit without fresh or waste water in the holding tanks but with automotive fluids such as fuel, oil, and radiator coolant.

Curbside - The side of the RV that would be at the curb when parked.

Detonation - Also known as "knock" or "ping," this is a condition in which some of the unburned air/fuel in the combustion chamber explodes at the wrong time in the ignition cycle, increasing mechanical and thermal stress on the engine.

Diesel Puller - Term for front engine diesel motor home.

Diesel Pusher – is a motor home with a rear diesel engine.

Dinette - booth-like dining area. Table usually drops to convert unit into a bed at night.

Dinghy - A vehicle towed behind a motor home, sometimes with two wheels on a special trailer called a tow dolly, but often with all four wheels on the ground.

Dry Camping/Boondocking -- camping in a recreational vehicle with no hookups and no utilities.

DSI Ignition - direct spark ignition - this term refers to the method of igniting the main burner on a propane fired appliance. The burner is lit with an electric spark and the flame is monitored by an electronic circuit board. This ignition system is used in refrigerators, furnaces and water heaters. There is now a version of stove tops that light the burners with a DSI ignition.

Dual Electrical System - RV equipped with lights, appliances which operate on 12-volt battery power when self-contained, and with a converter, on 110 AC current when in campgrounds or with an onboard generator.

Dually - A pickup truck, or light-duty tow vehicle, with four tires on one rear axle.

Ducted AC - is air conditioning supplied through a ducting system in the ceiling. This supplies cooling air at various vents located throughout the RV.

Ducted HEAT - is warm air from the furnace supplied to various locations in the RV through a ducting system located in the floor. (Similar to house heating systems)

Dump station - Usually a concrete pad with an inlet opening connected to an underground sewage system at a campground or other facility offering dumping service to RV travelers.

DW - Dry weight. The manufacturer's listing of the approximate weight of the RV with no supplies, water, fuel or passengers.

Engine Oil Cooler - A heat exchanger, similar to a small radiator, through which engine oil passes and is cooled by airflow.

Equalizing Hitch – is a hitch that utilizes spring bars that are placed under tension to distribute a portion of the trailer's hitch weight to the tow vehicle's front axle and the trailer's axles. The hitch is also known as a weight-distributing hitch.

Extended Stay Site -- Sites allotted for RVers to stay for an extended period of time, like a month or a season. Often times, parks that allow extended stays have restrictions against RVs that are more than 5 or 10 years old.

Federal Parks -- Parks run by the National Forest Service (NFS) or the National Park Service (NPS). These parks often offer work programs for reduced rate camping.

Fifth-Wheel Trailers - Fifth-wheel trailers are designed to be coupled to a special hitch that is mounted over the rear axle in the bed of a pickup truck. These trailers can have one, two or three axles and are the largest type of trailer built. Because of their special hitch requirements, fifth-wheel trailers can only be towed by trucks or specialized vehicles prepared for fifth-wheel trailer compatibility.

Final Drive Ratio – is the reduction ratio found in the gear set that is located farthest from the engine. This is the same as the axle ratio.

Fiver - Other name for fifth wheel.

FMCA - Abbreviation for Family Motor Coach Association.

Frame-Mount Hitch - Class II and higher hitches are designed to be bolted to the vehicle frame or cross members. This type of hitch may have a permanent ball mount, or may have a square-tube receiver into which a removable hitch bar or shank is installed.

Fresh water - Water suitable for human consumption.

Full hookup - Term for campground accommodations offering water, sewer/septic and electricity; also refers to a RV with the abilities to use 'full-hookups'.

Full-timing - Living in one's RV all year long. These RVers are known as full-timers.

Galley - The kitchen of an RV.

Gas Pusher - Slang for rear gasoline engine mounted chassis on motor home.

Gaucho - Sofa/dinette bench that converts into a sleeping unit; a term less used now than formerly.

GAWR (Gross Axle Weight Rating) - The manufacturer's rating for the maximum allowable weight that an axle is designed to carry. Gawr applies to tow vehicle, trailer, and fifth-wheel and motor home axles.

GCWR (Gross Combination Weight Rating) – is the maximum allowable weight of the combination of tow vehicle and trailer/ fifth-wheel, or motor home and dinghy. It includes the weight of the vehicle, trailer/fifth-wheel (or dinghy), cargo, passengers and a full load of fluids (fresh water, propane, fuel, etc.).

Gear Vendor - Brand name for an auxiliary transmission designed to give the driver control of the vehicle's gear ratio and being able to split gears for peak performance and at the same time have an overdrive.

Generator - An electrical device powered by gasoline or diesel fuel, and sometimes propane, for generating 120-volt AC power.

Genset - Abbreviation for generator set.

Gooseneck - A colloquial name for fifth-wheel travel trailers.

Gray water – is used water that drains from the kitchen and bathroom sinks and the shower into a holding tank, called a gray water holding tank that is located under the main floor of the RV.

Group Camping Areas -- Camping areas at a campground that accommodate larger groups of twenty or more. Typically group camping areas have a fire ring and/or other central location for group activities.

GTWR (Gross Trailer Weight Rating) - Maximum allowable weight of a trailer, fully loaded with cargo and fluids.

GVWR (Gross Vehicle Weight Rating) – is the total allowable weight of a vehicle, including passengers, cargo, fluids and hitch weight.

Hard-sided - RV walls made of aluminum or other hard surface.

Heat Exchanger - A heat exchanger is a device that transfers heat from one source to another. For example, there is a heat exchanger in your furnace - the propane flame and combustion products are contained inside the heat exchanger that is sealed from the inside area. Inside air is blown over the surface of the exchanger, where it is warmed and the blown through the ducting system for room heating. The combustion gases are vented to the outside air.

Heat Strip - A heat strip is an electric heating element located in the air conditioning system with the warm air distributed by the air conditioner fan and ducting system. They are typically 1500 watt elements (about the same wattage as an electric hair dryer) and have limited function. Basically they "take the chill off"

High Profile – is a fifth-wheel trailer with a higher-than-normal front to allow more than 6 feet of standing room inside the raised area.

Historic sites -- These are sites of national cultural importance. They include buildings, objects, monuments and landscapes. Historic sites are generally open to visitors.

Hitch - The fastening unit that joins a movable vehicle to the vehicle that pulls it.

Hitch Weight - The amount of weight imposed on the hitch when the trailer/fifth-wheel is coupled. Sometimes it is referred to as conventional trailer "tongue weight." Hitch weight for a travel trailer can be 10-15 percent of overall weight; fifth-wheel hitch weight is usually 18 to 20 percent of the overall weight.

Holding Tanks - Tanks that retain waste water when the RV unit is not connected to a sewer. The gray water tank holds wastewater from the sinks and shower; the black water tank holds sewage from the toilet.

Hookups - The ability of connecting to a campground's facilities. The major types of hookups are electrical, water and sewer. If all three of these hookups are available, it is termed full hookup. Hookups may also include telephone and cable TV in some campgrounds.

House Battery - Battery or batteries in motor home for operating the 12-volt system within the motor home, separate from the chassis.

HP - Abbreviation for "horse power".

HR - Abbreviation for Holiday Rambler, a well-known RV manufacturer.

Hula skirt - Term used for a type of dirt skirt accessory some RVers use on the back of their motor home to aid in the protection from debris thrown from their rear wheels to the vehicles directly behind them or being towed behind them. This dirt skirt is usually the length of the rear bumper and resembles a 'short' version of a Hawaiian 'hula-skirt', hence the term.

Inverter - A unit that changes 12-volt direct current to 110-volt alternating current to allow operation of computers, TV sets, and such when an RV is not hooked up to electricity.

Island Queen – is a queen-sized bed with walking space on both sides.

Jackknife - 90% angle obtained from turning/backing fifth wheel or travel trailer with tow vehicle. Jackknifing a short bed truck towing a fifth wheel without the use of a slider hitch or extended fifth wheel pin box can result in damage to the truck cab or breaking out the back window of the truck cab from the truck and fifth wheel "colliding".

KOA - Kampgrounds of America, a franchise chain of RV parks in North America that offers camping facilities to vacationers and overnighters.

Laminate - sandwich of structural frame members, wall paneling, insulation and exterior covering, adhesive-bonded under pressure and/or heat to form the RVs walls, floor and/or roof.

Leveling - Positioning the RV in camp so it will be level, using ramps (also called levelers) placed under the wheels, built-in scissors jacks, or power leveling jacks.

Limited-Slip Differential - A differential that is designed with a mechanism that limits the speed and torque differences between its two outputs, ensuring that torque is distributed to both drive wheels, even when one is on a slippery surface.

Livability Packages – are the items to equip a motor home for daily living, which may be rented at nominal cost from rental firm, rather than brought from home. Include bed linens, pillows and blankets, bath towels, pots and pans, kitchen utensils, cutlery.

Log Cabins -- Typically two or more rooms, and accommodates four or more people. Cabins usually have private bathrooms and a kitchen area with a refrigerator.

LP Gas - Propane; abbreviation for liquefied petroleum gas, which is a gas liquefied by compression, consisting of flammable hydrocarbons and obtained as a by-product from the refining of petroleum or natural gas. Also called bottled gas, LPG (liquid petroleum gas) and CPG (compressed petroleum gas).

Marine parks -- These are unique and outstanding marine areas set aside to conserve seawater plants and animals. They're divided into zones that allow different, sustainable levels of commercial and recreational activities.

MH - Abbreviation for "motor home".

Minnie Winnie - A brand model of Winnebago.

Motor coach – is the term for motor home on "bus-type" chassis.

NADA - Abbreviation for National Automotive Dealers Association.

Nature reserves --These are areas of special scientific interest, set up mainly to conserve their native plant and animal communities. Few have visitor facilities.

NCC (Net Carrying Capacity) – is the maximum weight of all passengers (if applicable), personal belongings, food, fresh water, supplies -- derived by subtracting the UVW from the GVWR.

Nonpotable water - Water not suitable for human consumption.

OEM - Original Equipment Manufacturer.

Park Model - Type of RV that is usually designed for permanent parking but is shorter in length than a traditional mobile home. All the amenities of a mobile home but not built for recreational travel.

Part-timers - People who use their RV for longer than normal vacation time but less than one year.

Patio mat - Carpet or woven mat for use on ground outside of RV. It may be used whether or not a concrete patio pad is available where camping.

Payload Capacity - The maximum allowable weight that can be placed in or on a vehicle, including cargo, passengers, fluids and fifth-wheel or conventional hitch loads.

Pilot - a pilot is a small standby flame that is used to light the main burner of a propane fired appliance when the thermostat calls for heat. Pilots can be used in furnaces, water heaters, refrigerators, ovens and stove tops.

Pitch-in - Term for a RV campground "get-together", usually means "pitching-in" a covered dish or casserole.

PO - Abbreviation for "pop-up" camper.

Pop-out - Term for room or area that 'pops-out' for additional living space in RV. This type of expanded living area was more common before the technology of slide-out rooms became popular and available.

Popup/Pop-Up - Folding camping trailer.

Porpoising - A term used to define an up and down motion with a RV.

Primitive camping - Also known as "dry camping", boondocking. Camping without the modern convenience of full-hookup facilities of city/well water, sewer/septic and electricity. Primitive campers rely on 'on-board' systems for these conveniences; generator, batteries, stored water, etc.

Propane - LPG, or liquefied petroleum gas, used in RVs for heating, cooking and refrigeration. Also called bottle gas, for manner in which it is sold and stored.

Puller - slang for front engine motor home. Term most often used to refer to front mounted diesel engine motor homes.

Pull-through - A campsite that allows the driver to pull into the site to park, then pull out the other side when leaving, without ever having to back up.

Pusher - Slang for rear engine motor home. Term most often used to refer to diesel engine motor   homes.

Receiver - The portion of a hitch that permits a hitch bar or shank to be inserted. The receiver may be either 11/2-, 15/8- or 2-inch square; the smallest being termed a mini-hitch.

Reefer - Slang for "refrigerator". Refrigerators are often found in either a "two way" or "three way" operating mode. Two way: has a gas mode and an AC mode. Three way: has a gas mode, AC mode, and 12v DC mode. The coolant used in RV refrigeration is ammonia. The two most common manufacturers of RV refrigerators are Norcold and Dometic.

Regional parks -- Near large population centers, these parks offer open space and recreational and cultural opportunities for urban residents.

RIG - what many RVers call their units.

Road Wander - Term used to describe a lack of ability to maintain the motor home in a straight, forward travel without constant back and forth motion of the steering wheel.

Roof Air Conditioning - For most RVs, the air conditioning unit is mounted on the roof. Some RVs have "bus a/c" that is contained in a basement storage area.

RV - short for Recreation Vehicle, a generic term for all pleasure vehicles which contain living accommodations. Multiple units are RVs and persons using them are RVers.

RVDA - Abbreviation for Recreational Vehicle Dealer's Association.

RVIA - Abbreviation for Recreational Vehicle Industry Association.

RV Park -- Almost always privately owned, caters to overnight or seasonal guests who have recreational vehicles.

RV Resort Park -- Almost always privately owned, caters to overnight or seasonal guests who have recreational vehicles. RV Resort is often an indication of a well-developed, higher end park, but since any RV Park can call itself an RV Resort; this is not always the case.

Safety Chains - A set of chains that are attached to the trailer A-frame and must be connected to the tow vehicle while towing. Safety chains are intended to keep the trailer attached to the tow vehicle in the event of hitch failure, preventing the trailer from complete separation. They should be installed using an X-pattern, so the coupler is held off the road in the event of a separation.

Screen room - Term for screen enclosure that attaches to the exterior of a RV for a "bug free" outside sitting area. Some screen rooms have a canvas type roof for rain protection as well.

Self-contained - An RV that needs no external connections to provide short-term cooking, bathing, and heating functions and could park overnight anywhere.

Shank - Also called a hitch bar or stinger, the shank is a removable portion of the hitch system that carries the ball or adjustable ball mount, and slides into the receiver.

Shore cord - The external electrical cord that connects the vehicle to a campground electrical hookup.

Shore Power - Electricity provided to the RV by an external source other than the RV battery.

Slide-in - Term for a type of camper that mounts on a truck bed, because often this type of camper "slides-in" to the truck bed.

Slide-out - Additional living space that "slides-out" either by hydraulics, electricity or manually, when the RV is setup for camping.

Slider - Slang for slider-hitch.

Slider-hitch - Refers to a sliding hitch used on short bed trucks for enabling them to tow fifth wheels, allowing them sufficient clearance to jack-knife the trailer.

Snowbird - Term for someone in a northern climate that heads "south" in winter months.

Soft-sides - Telescoping side panels on an RV that can be raised or lowered usually constructed of canvas or vinyl and mesh netting.

Spring Bar - Component parts of a weight-distributing hitch system, the spring bars are installed and tensioned in such a manner as to distribute a portion of the trailer's hitch weight to the front axle of the tow vehicle and to the axles of the trailer.

State Park -- These parks, run by state facilities, have many recreation opportunities and/or visitor centers. They are set within an extensive scenic setting.

State Wayside -- Rest stops providing parking areas and restroom facilities with limited or no recreational opportunities.

State conservation areas -- These are parks, often containing important natural environments, which have been set aside mainly for outdoor recreation.

Stinger - See shank.

Street side - The part of the vehicle on the street side when parked.

Sway - Fishtailing action of the trailer caused by external forces that set the trailer's mass into a lateral (side-to-side) motion. The trailer's wheels serve as the axis or pivot point. This is also known as "yaw."

Sway Control - Devices designed to damp the swaying action of a trailer, either through a friction system or a "cam action" system that slows and absorbs the pivotal articulating action between tow vehicle and trailer.

Tail Swing – Motor homes built on chassis with short wheelbases and long overhangs behind the rear axle are susceptible to tail swing when turning sharply. As the motor home moves in reverse or turns a corner, the extreme rear of the coach can move horizontally and strike objects nearby (typically road signs and walls). Drivers need to be aware of the amount of tail swing in order to prevent accidents.

Tail gunner – is the end RV or vehicle in a caravan.

Telescoping - Compacting from front to back and/or top to bottom to make the living unit smaller for towing and storage.

Tent Sites -- no utilities, allows tent campers only.

Thermocouple - a thermocouple is a device that monitors the pilot flame of a pilot model propane appliance. If the pilot flame is extinguished the thermocouple causes the gas valve to shut off the flow of gas to both the pilot flame and the main burner.

Three-way refrigerators – These are appliances that can operate on a 12-volt battery, propane, or 110-volt electrical power.

Tip-out - Term for room (generally in older RVs) that "tipped-out" for additional living space once RV was parked. Newer RVs mainly use 'slide-out' rooms.

Toad – Another name for the towed vehicle.

Toe - Wheel alignment - Toe is the measure of whether the front of the wheels (looking down from the top) are closer (toe-in) or farther (toe-out) than the back of the wheels.

Tongue Weight - The amount of weight imposed on the hitch when the trailer is coupled. See "hitch weight."

Tow Bar - A device used for connecting a dinghy vehicle to the motor home when it's towed with all four wheels on the ground.

Tow Rating - The manufacturer's rating of the maximum weight limit that can safely be towed by a particular vehicle. Tow ratings are related to overall trailer weight, not trailer size, in most cases. However, some tow ratings impose limits as to frontal area of the trailer and overall length. The vehicle manufacturer according to several criteria, including engine size, transmission, axle ratio, brakes, chassis, cooling systems and other special equipment, determines tow ratings.

Tow car - A car towed by an RV to be used as transportation when the RV is parked in a campground.

Toy-hauler - Term for fifth wheel, travel trailer or motor home with built-in interior cargo space for motorcycles, bikes, etc.

Trailer Brakes - Brakes that are built into the trailer axle systems and are activated either by electric impulse or by a surge mechanism. The overwhelming majority of RVs utilize electric trailer brakes that are actuated when the tow vehicle's brakes are operated, or when a brake controller is manually activated. Surge brakes utilize a mechanism that is positioned at the coupler that detects when the tow vehicle is slowing or stopping, and activates the trailer brakes via a hydraulic system (typically used on boats).

Transmission Cooler - A heat exchanger similar to a small radiator through which automatic transmission fluid passes and is cooled by airflow.

Travel Trailer - Also referred to as "conventional trailers," these types of rigs have an A-frame and coupler and are attached to a ball mount on the tow vehicle. Travel trailers are available with one, two or three axles. Depending upon tow ratings, conventional trailers can be towed by trucks, cars or sport-utility vehicles.

Triple towing - Term for three vehicles attached together. This is usually a tow vehicle pulling a fifth wheel and the fifth wheel pulling a boat.

TV - Abbreviation for "tow vehicle".

Umbilical Cord - The wiring harness that connects the tow vehicle to the trailer, supplying electricity to the trailer's clearance and brake lights, electric brakes and a 12-volt DC power line to charge the trailer's batteries. An umbilical cord can also be the power cable that is used to connect to campground 120-volt AC electrical hookups.

Underbelly - The RVs under floor surface, which is protected by a weatherproofed material.

UTQGL (Uniform Tire Quality Grade Labeling) - A program that is directed by the government to provide consumers with information about three characteristics of the tire: tread wear, traction and temperature. Following government prescribed test procedures, tire manufacturers perform their own evaluations for these characteristics. Each manufacturer then labels the tire, according to grade.

UVW (Unloaded Vehicle Weight) - Weight of the vehicle without manufacturer's or dealer-installed options and before adding fuel, water or supplies.

Wagonmaster - A leader, either hired or chosen, who guides a caravan of recreational vehicles on a trip. The wagonmaster usually makes advance reservations for campgrounds, shows, cruises, sightseeing and group meals.

Wally World - Slang term used by RVers to describe a Wal-Mart.

Weekender's - People who own their RVs for weekend and vacation use.

Weight-Carrying Hitch - Also known as a "dead-weight" hitch, this category includes any system that accepts the entire hitch weight of the trailer. In the strictest sense, even a weight-distributing hitch can act as a load-carrying hitch if the spring bars are not installed and placed under tension.

Weight-Distributing Hitch - Also known as an "equalizing" hitch, this category includes hitch systems that utilize spring bars that can be placed under tension to distribute a portion of the trailer's hitch weight to the tow vehicle's front axle and the trailer's axles.

Weights: - water (weight): 8.3 lbs. per gallon; LP gas (weight): 4.5 lbs. per gallon; Gasoline: weighs 6.3 pounds per gallon; Diesel fuel: weighs 6.6 pounds per gallon; Propane: weighs 4.25 pounds per gallon.

Wet Weight - Term used by RVers to describe the weight of a RV with all storage and holding tanks full. i.e., water, propane, etc.

Wheelbase - Distance between center lines of the primary axles of a vehicle. If a motor home includes a tag axle, the distance is measured from the front axle to the center point between the drive and tag axles.

Wide body - Designs that stretch RVs from the traditional 96-inch width to 100 or 102 inches.

Wilderness -- Wilderness is usually an 'overlay' on national parks or reserves. Wilderness areas are large, remote and essentially unchanged by modern human activity. They are managed so that native plant and animal communities are disturbed as little as possible.

Winnie - Nickname for Winnebago, a well-known RV manufacturer.

Winterize - To prepare the RV for winter use or storage.

World Heritage-listed areas -- The globally recognized World Heritage list contains some of the most important examples of natural and cultural heritage in the world. More than 600 precious places are on the list, from the Great Barrier Reef to the pyramids of Egypt.

Yaw - Fishtailing action of the trailer caused by external forces that set the trailer's mass into a lateral (side-to-side) motion. The trailer's wheels serve as the axis or pivot point. This is also known as "sway."

Yurts -- circular, domed tent-like structures with wood floors, electricity, heating, lockable doors and sleeping accommodations for typically for four or more people.

Made in the USA
Lexington, KY
10 September 2014